**Brigadier General
Theodore G. Shuey**

Omaha Beach

Field Guide

HEIMDAL

Forword

It is truly a privilege to work with Georges Bernage and Heimdal Publishing in creating this guide to the events which occurred on Omaha Beach on D-Day. Having visited the site for fifteen years, the previous Heimdal works were critical to my understanding of the action on 6 June 1944. All of the tours I have conducted for American groups over the years were based on this excellent research.

The following text includes over 100 quotes taken from members of practically every American unit which landed on Omaha Beach the morning of D-Day. The perspective of each man was obviously influenced by the time and position in which they landed, but the horror they experienced was very similar expressed.

I especially appreciate the hospitality of the Clemençon family at the Hotel du Casino and the assistance of Madame Le Gallois at La Plage d'Or. Her family owned the Hotel and donated the land for the National Guard Memorial.

The detailed information provided by Martin-Robert Galle, grandson of Oberst Ernst Goth commanding Grenadier Regiment 916, 352nd Infantry Division was extremely helpful. In addition, first hand accounts provided by Lutz Heinz, son of Lieutenant Hans Heinz who led the counterattack effort against the Americans were invaluable.

I greatly appreciate the information made available by the Brissard family at the Musee D.Day Omaha in Vierville. Catherine Chartier and Daniel Tréfeu at the Musee Memorial d'Omaha Beach in St. Laurent were very helpful and their affection for the 29th Infantry Division is greatly appreciated. In addition, Superintendent Hans Hooker and the entire staff of the American Cemetery could not have been more helpful.

The knowledge and resources of the Big Red One Museum in Colleville and Pierre-Louis Gosselin were very important to my research, as was Paul Herbert, staff of the First Division Museum in Cantigny, Illinois.

I am grateful to the commune of Vierville-sur-mer, Mayor Antoine de Bellaigue and his deputy and former Mayor Jean-Marie Oxéant for their support.

I owe a great deal to Céline Lautour who served as my primary translator and assistant in France. Her fluent French and German were invaluable. Also most important was the work of my good friend David Ashe. His remarkable photography and assistance in the exploration of the German defenses was extremely important to the end product.

The clerical and administrative assistance of Anna Diehl Davis was critical and much appreciated. As always my wife, Elizabeth, was a great help in editing and enduring countless trips across Normandy to support my efforts.

- Ouvrage écrit par le *Brigadier General* Theodore Shuey
- Conception et maquette : Georges Bernage

- Mise en pages : Christel Lebret
- Traduction française : Céline Lautour

Editions Heimdal
BP 61350 - 14406 BAYEUX Cedex
Tél. : 02.31.51.68.68 - Fax : 02.31.51.68.60 - E-mail : Editions.Heimdal@wanadoo.fr
site internet : www.editions-heimdal.fr

ISBN 978-2-84048-371-7

The Golden Beach

Upon America's entry into World War II, the Allied staff intensified their effort to create the very complex and detailed plan to begin the liberation of Western Europe from German occupation. The resulting product would become known as "Operation Overlord." There were a number of sub plans particularly in the area of deception, such as Operation Fortitude and Operation Glimmer, but assault phase of the invasion would be identified as "Operation Neptune." It encompassed the landings originally set for invasion day, D-Day, June 5, 1944. The planned assault focused on the Norman Coast of France and the Bay of the Seine. The critical beach which was to connect the American and British invasion forces was designated as "Sector O" for Omaha and would become famous as "Omaha Beach." This five-mile stretch of sand was known to the French as *la Plage d'or*, "the golden beach." Allied success or failure on D-Day would hang in the balance during the struggle here that would create another name for the site, "Bloody Omaha."

Using the military phonetic alphabet, Sector Omaha began on the east bank of the Vire River estuary with Sector "A" for Able, which included the town of Isigny, then "B" for Baker and the fishing village of Grandcamp, with "C" Charlie encompassing the cliffs of Pointe du Hoc and Pointe de la Percee. Sectors "Dog," "Easy," and "Fox" targeted "the golden beach," the beautiful flat, open stretch of sand, which had been a French resort area prior to World War II. Section "G" Golf, included the cliffs from Omaha Beach east to Port en Bessin. Each sector was additionally divided by colors that designated the eight actual landing beaches.

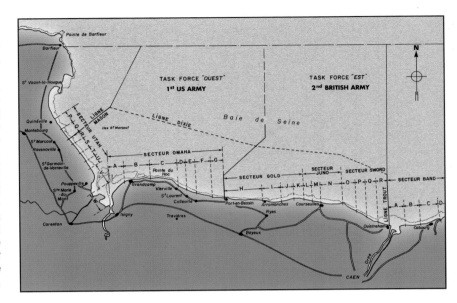

The only possible landing site for a divisional sized unit of infantry in "Sector O" was the wide expanse of "the golden beach." A short distance beyond the beach the ground rises abruptly from 100 to 175 feet in height. To the west, just beyond of the town of Vierville-sur-Mer, were the cliffs of "Sector Charlie" with identical heights to the east in "Sector Golf, "beginning just below the town of Sainte-Honorine-des-Pertes. "Omaha Beach" was wide enough to accommodate an infantry assault force on broad front, but attacking the cliffs would require special skill units.

Plan of the beach sectors allotted to the two allied armies. Rigorous organization directed the thousands of men to the right place. One can see here the Omaha sector subdivided into landing sectors Charlie, Dog, Easy and Fox. (Map by Heimdal)

A very strong easterly current creates « runnels » or deep cuts in the sand. (David Ashe.)

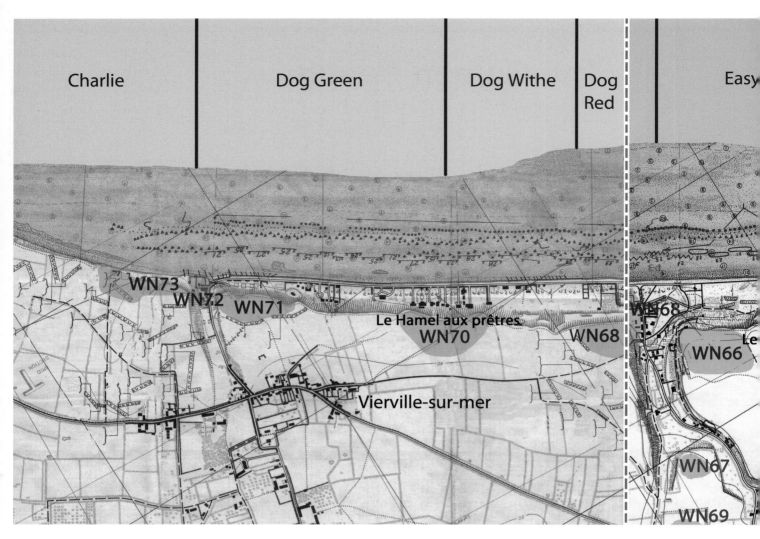

Charlie | Dog Green | Dog Withe | Dog Red | Easy

WN73
WN72
WN71
Le Hamel aux prêtres
WN70
WN68
WN68
WN66
Le
Vierville-sur-mer
WN67
WN69

Villages, coast road and German strongpoints. (Heimdal.)

Omaha Beach would provide the perfect location for the artificial harbor planned to support the American advance inland. The location would serve as the critical link between the British and Canadian invasion sites to the east, which began at the Orne River, and the American "Utah Beach" to the west. The English Channel tides on Omaha Beach are the second fastest in the world. At low tide, the water recedes to as far out as 400 yards from the seawall. At the low tide mark the water begins to rise slowly at first, only an inch in the first hour, but in the second hour the depth here reaches seven feet, then up to eighteen feet at high tide. As it rises, a very strong easterly current creates "runnels" or deep cuts in the sand. The resulting sandbars become natural obstacles for landing craft.

Leading inland from Omaha Beach were five openings, which had been created through generations of erosion, as water from the fields and streams above, made their way into the Bay of the Seine. Overlord planners identified these critical routes off of the beach as "Draw," because they resembled the gulleys or cuts in the high ground of the American western states. The draws would be recognized as D-1 below Vierville-sur-mer, which was the only paved road leading from the beach. Then there was D-3 with a cluster of houses at its base known as Les Moulins. Further east was E-1, the Ruquet Valley leading to the town of St. Laurent-sur-mer. "Sur-Mer" identified a village as being "within sight of the water" or "on the

sea." The remaining two draws to the east were E-3 leading to Colleville and F-1 which rose inland to the village of Cabourg.

The western half of "Sector O" had a seawall that protected the beach road that connected St. Laurent to Vierville. Scattered between the road and the steep cliffs overlooking the beach were several houses and summer cottages. Near the Les Moulins Draw, wooden breakwaters extended onto the beach. The area behind the beach further east was relatively flat with some grass, even a swampy area. The Ruquet Valley had few structures, just flat open beach and sand dunes.

While the high ground facing the Bay of the Seine dominated Omaha Beach, inland the ground was relatively flat and dotted with tiny farms. This was the *bocage*, the Norman word for fields and woods, divided by the famous "hedgerows" that had been used for centuries to divide the farms. The hedgerow was a high bank with a base of earth and rock with dense shrubs or trees on the top. The first use of this method to divide farm fields dates back 4000-6000 years to the Neolithic Age.

An average of 1,300 yards of fields and orchards separated the cliffs from a coastal road that ran parallel to the beach and connected the small Norman coastal villages inland. Three miles farther south from the coast road was a more improved route running between the larger towns of Caen in the east and Carentan to the west. Allied plan-

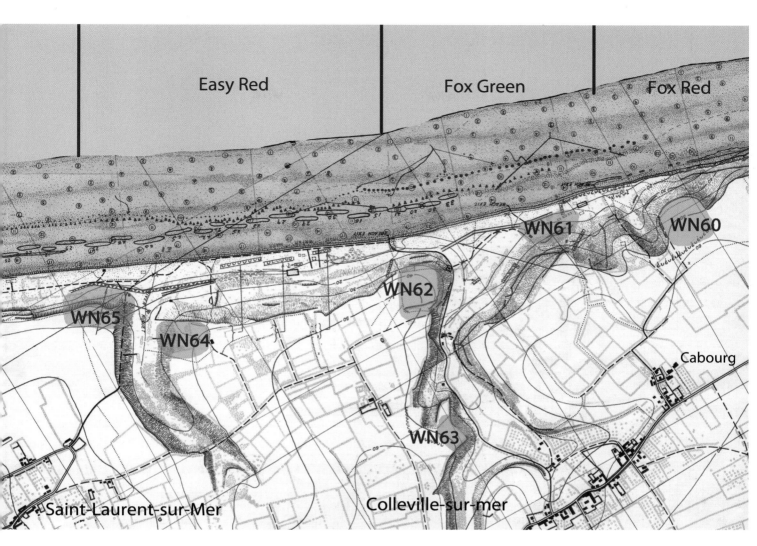

Easy Red   Fox Green   Fox Red

WN61

WN60

WN62

WN65

WN64

Cabourg

WN63

Saint-Laurent-sur-Mer

Colleville-sur-mer

ners would identify this route as the "lateral road." This road constituted the D-Day objective for the units landing on Omaha Beach.

An examination of the terrain of Omaha Beach clearly reveals that in military terms it favors the defenders. The high ground above the beach provided an exceptional position to observe and engage any effort to land during either high or low tide. The five draws spread across the five miles of beach created a natural exit from the beach and channelized any assault force into an easily defended narrow route.

In early June as D-Day approached, the Allies began loading the ships in preparation for D-Day. A storm would delay their departure by one day, but in the early morning hours of June 5, Supreme Allied Commander, General Dwight D. Eisenhower, issued the final order setting Operation Overlord into action. D-Day would be the following morning, June 6, 1944. General Eisenhower's D-Day message read to the soldiers as they crossed the English Channel began:

"Soldiers, Sailors, and Airmen of the Allied Expeditionary Force! You are about to embark upon a great crusade, toward which we have striven these many months. The eyes of the world are upon you. The hopes and prayers of liberty loving people everywhere march with you."

He would close his message: *"I have full confidence in your courage, devotion to duty and skill in battle. We will accept nothing less than full vic-*

tory. Good luck! And let us all beseech the blessings of Almighty God upon this great and noble undertaking."

Operation Neptune

Operation Overlord assigned Sector Utah and Sector Omaha to the American First United States Army, commanded by Lieutenant General Omar Bradley. The planned assault into Utah would be the responsibility of VII Corps led by its 4th Infantry Division. The right flank of the invasion force would be secured by American 82nd and 101st Airborne Divisions, which would be dropped behind Utah Beach during the night before the landings. Omaha Beach, the critical sector between Utah and the British 50th Division landing on "Gold Beach," was the responsibility of the V Corps under the command of Major General Leonard Gerow. He was a graduate of the Virginia Military Institute (VMI), and had commanded the 29th Division from 16 February 1943 until moving to Corps Command, 17 July 1943.

Another VMI graduate, General George Marshall, the Chief of Staff of the U. S. Army, held him in high regard and their relationship helped shape the landing plan for Omaha Beach. There can be little doubt the two Generals had a great deal of influence on the selection units from the National Guard's Virginia based 29th Division to have a major role in the D-Day landings. In order to maximize command and control, normal planning would have assigned two regiments of a division to the assault, with the third regiment landing in reserve.

The units of ground "Force O" were built around the U. S. Army's veteran 1st Infantry Division with combat experience from landings in North Africa, Sicily and Italy. It was commanded by Major General Clarence Huebner and consisted of three experienced Regimental Combat Teams; (RCTs), the 16th, 18th, and 26th. They would be responsible for the assault into a portion of Easy and Fox Beach sectors. Landing simultaneously would be three Regimental Combat Teams of the 29th Division, the 116th from Virginia and the 115th and 175th from Maryland. They would be responsible for section Dog with the very critical Vierville Draw and the western portion of Easy. The landings would also include the 2nd and 5th Ranger Battalions assigned the difficult task of scaling the cliffs in sector Charlie.

In an unusual command and control configuration, on D-Day, Lieutenant General Bradley placed the three 29th Division Regimental Combat Teams under the command of General Huebner initially. They would be attached to the 1st Division for the landings, and later released at a time determined by V Corps. His Assistant Division Commander (ADC), Brigadier General Willard Wyman, and the staff of the 1st Division would be in command on the beach. Brigadier General Norman Cota, ADC of the 29th Division, would also land and assist his subordinate units in the landings. The 29th Division units were projected to be released to their commander, Major General Charles Gerhardt, twenty-four hours after the landings.

The **1st Division** was a unit of the regular United States Army. It became the "First Division" as part of the restructuring which occurred in 1917 during the Army's preparation for the deployments to France as part of America's World War I Expeditionary Force. It was easily recognized by its distinctive "Big Red One" patch and was the first American unit deployed to England in World War II. Their motto was "No Mission Too Difficult, No Sacrifice Too Great—Duty First." The Division recognized the challenges related to the landings scheduled to occur at H-Hour of D-Day, 0630. Their 16th RCT that had landed first in both North Africa and Sicily would lead the first wave in assaulting sectors "Easy" and "Fox." They would be followed by the 18th RCT and the 26th RCT. After establishing a beachhead, the 1st Division was tasked to move inland straight south and to link with the British 50th Infantry Division coming off of Gold Beach to the east.

Major-General Clarence R Huebner (Commander of the 1st Infantry Division) reporting on the positions of his division at a conference with General Eisenhower. (NA/coll Heimdal).

Shoulder patch worn on the top of the left sleeve by the men of the 29th Division. (Doc. Heimdal)

Cloth patch of the 1st Infantry Division, "the Big Red One" worn on the top of the left shoulder of the uniform jacket.

General Eisenhower and Major-General Gerhardt.

The **29th Division's 116th RCT** would lead the first wave on the western portion of Omaha Beach designated "Dog," followed by the 115th RCT and the 175th RCT. The first wave would focus its 1st Battalion, landing a company at a time, on opening the very critical Vierville Draw, Exit D-1. Three companies of the 2nd Battalion would assault other objectives in Dog and Easy. The 29th Division, known as the "Blue and Gray" Division, was composed of National Guard units from states that sided with either the north or south during the American Civil War, 1861-1865. Their patch blended the colors blue, representing the north or Union, and gray, representing the south or Confederacy, in the design of the Korean symbol of life, the yin and yang. Their motto was "29 Let's Go!" After seizing their initial objectives, the 29th Division was to turn west down the coast road to link with the Rangers on Pointe du Hoc, then proceed to the fishing village of Isigny. There they would meet the 4th Infantry Division and Airborne units coming inland from sector Utah.

Cloth patch of the Rangers.

Commanders of the 116th, the Division's assault regiment. Left to right: Colonel Canham, CO; Lt. Col. Lawrence E. Meeks, 3d Battalion; Lt. Col. John A. Metcalfe, 1st Battalion; Major Sidney V. Bingham, 2d Battalion.

Two American Ranger Battalions were also to play a critical role in the assault on Omaha Beach. They were organized into three groups. Force A was comprised of Company's D, E, and F of Lieutenant Colonel James Rudder's 2nd Battalion, and were assigned the assault on the cliffs in Sector Charlie known as Pointe du Hoc. Force B, Company's A and C of the 2nd Battalion, commanded by Captain Ralph Goranson, was to land on the extreme eastern edge of Charlie, and assault the Vierville Draw and the cliffs known as Pointe de la Percee. Force C, comprised of the 5th Rangers under Lieutenant Colonel Max Schneider, was to follow Force A at Pointe du Hoc if they received the message "Praise the Lord", which meant success had been achieved there. If the message was "tilt", or there was no response, it would mean failure. In that event, Task Force C would shift to their alternate assignment, which was to follow and support the 29th Division in Dog Sector and then move to Point du Hoc by land. Force B would land to their right and provide flank security initially, then accompany them to destroy the guns at Pointe du Hoc.

Rear Admiral John Hall, Jr. commanded naval Task Force 124 or "Force O". It was his responsibility to deliver 34,142 soldiers and 3,306 vehicles onto Omaha Beach on D-Day. It consisted of 700 ships, plus attached landing craft designed to carry the soldiers and equipment of V Corps onto Omaha Beach. As it moved south across the 120 miles of the English Channel separating England from the Norman coast of France, the night of 5 June 1944, it was preceded by minesweepers to clear lanes for the invasion force. Destroyer Squadron 18, led by the USS Frankford, screened the flotilla's movement, preventing any interference from German U-Boats or E-Boats.

Arriving off the Norman coast around 0300, Force O would anchor in the Bay of the Seine, twelve miles off the beach. It was comprised of a Bom-

Some officers of the 1st Battalion, 116th Regiment in England. In the back row left to right are: Capt. Taylor N. Fellers, Bedford, Virginia, Company A; Capt. Ettore V. Zappacosta, Philadelphia, Pennsylvania, Company B; 2nd Lt. James J. Limber, Chicago, Illinois, Headquarters Company, 1st Lt. Alfred S. Anderson, Long Island, New York, Company A; and Capt. Berthier B. Hawks, Lawreceville, Virginia, Company C. In the front row left to right are Lt. Donald P. Casapulla, New Jersey, Company A, and 1st Lt. Vincent P. Labowicz, Massachusetts, Company D. Of the seven officers, Fellers, Zappacosta, Limber, Anderson, and Labowicz were all killed on D-day. Hawks was wounded. (Courtesy of Donald P. Casapulla.)

bardment Force, the Landing Element, and a Close Gunfire Support Group. Admiral C. F. Bryant commanded the bombardment group, built around the battleships USS Texas and USS Arkansas. There were four light cruisers; two were the FFS (Free French Ships) Georges Leygues and Montcalm, plus the British HMS Bellona and Glasgow. There were twelve American destroyers of the 36th Destroyer Division. Commanded by Commander W. J. Marshall, it consisted of the USS Baldwin, Carmick, Doyle, Emmons, Frankfort, Harding,

The commander of Force O, Rear Admiral Hall's flagship, the USS Ancon, also served as a floating headquarters for Major-General Gerow, commanding V Corps, Major-General Huebner, in command of 1st Infantry Div. and Brig.-Gen William M Hoge of the Engineer Special Brigade. Launched in 1938 she was essentially a passenger liner until requisitioned by the Army in 1943 for service as a troopship. The following year she was converted as a headquarters ship for amphibious operations. With a crew of 707 men and armed with two five pounder guns, four 50mm and fourteen 20mm, she took part in the landings on Sicily and at Salerno before flying the flag of the Eleventh Amphibious Force. Under the command of Cmdr. Mead S Pearson, the Ancon sailed from Portland on 5 June and dropped anchor 0251 on 6 June, 22km off Omaha beach. This modern headquarters ship remained offshore until D+21 when she returned to England before taking part in the Okinawa landings. On this photo she is seen on the right, anchored off Omaha Beach on 7 June. (National Archives).

USS Thompson. (NA)

McCook, Melbreak, Satterlee, Talybont, Tanatside, and Thompson. Allied intelligence had identified numerous German strong points, "SPs," the Bombardment Force would engage for thirty minutes before H-Hour. For years the British had mapped Hitler's Atlantic Wall and classified their efforts as "BIGOT," (British Invasion of German Occupied Territory). Access to BIGOT plans required a security clearance of its own, one level above American "Top Secret."

The assault element of Admiral Hall's Landing Group was comprised of seven ships, carrying the soldiers of the first waves and many of their landing craft and eight LSIs (Landing Ship Infantry) with both troops and equipment. These large vessels would be offloaded at sea. There were thirty-three Landing Craft Infantry (LCIs), which could land two hundred or more soldiers directly onto the beach. There were smaller landing craft which carried up to thirty-four. There were eighteen British LCAs (Landing Craft Armored or Assault) and twenty-six American LCVPs, Landing Craft Vehicle and Personnel, commonly known as the Higgins Boat named for its builder in New Orleans, Andrew Jackson Higgins. The first wave on Omaha Beach would land in a combination of these forty-four small craft.

In a decision later questioned, Allied planners chose not to utilize the American "Amtrac" landing craft, the amphibious tracked vehicle that had been so successful in the Pacific theater in assaults against the Japanese held islands. Over three hundred of these tracked landing craft had been sent to England. They would have allowed the first waves of V Corps to land and work through the obstacles to the seawall. Major General Charles Corlett, who had joined the American Army in England and would become the XIX Corps commander after D-Day, had seen the effectiveness of the landing craft in the Pacific. He apprised both General Eisenhower and Lieutenant General Bradley of the protection the amtrac could provide soldiers landing on the sandy French beaches on D-Day. His recommendation, however, fell on deaf ears, and Americans coming in at low tide would have to disembark their landing craft and cross the open beach on foot.

TF "O" also had twenty-four LSTs (Landing Ship Tank), the largest equipment carrier, and a hundred and forty-seven LCTs (Landing Craft Tank), which would carry three to four tracked vehicles to the beach in the first waves. In addition, there were thirty-three support vessels. The landing craft would be loaded, most before 0430, and circle in Assembly Area "Elder" until the entire assault group was ready to go in. Then they would move south to their LD (Line of Departure) to prepare to attack in "waves." The landing craft for the 16th RCT would assemble in Area Ohio in front of the eastern beaches of Easy and Fox, while the 116th RCT would form up in Area Oregon off Dog.

The Close Gunfire Support Group commanded by Captain L. S. Sabin was built around the LCT platform, which had been modified to serve in a number of fire support roles. There were nine LCTs (Rocket) each carrying one thousand sixty-four 5" rockets on their decks and five LCG (Gun) boats had two 4.7 inch naval guns and two 25 pounder British made howitzers. These boats would precede the first wave assault boats and attempt to neutralize any German positions remaining on the beach. The unforeseen difficulty was the choppy waters the morning of D-Day. The bouncing flat-bottomed boats caused the rockets or rounds to either land short in the water or go long and over the cliffs. There were also the LCFs (Flak) armed with 20mm anti-aircraft guns and even LCTs to generate smoke to cover the fleet and the landings.

At 0530, "Operation Neptune" was triggered with the Eighth Air Force, under the command of the infamous Lieutenant General James Doolittle, scheduled to bomb Omaha Beach in advance of the infantry landings. The 75 squadrons of Second Bomb Division, each with 6 heavy Liberator bombers, would strike preplanned targets on Omaha Beach. Flying north to south, the 450 planes would drop 1,300, primarily 100 lb. bombs, to carpet the German defenses. In addition to the destruction of the defenses, the bombing would create a "moonscape" of craters in the sand to provide protection for the first waves of Ameri-

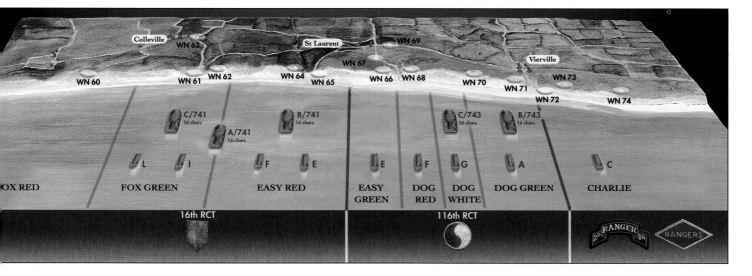

The planned landings on Omaha beach. The strength of the currents decided otherwise. (graphic by Heimdal).

Landing Craft technical specifications

LCM. This barge could carry a Sherman tank or other vehicles, up to 32 tons, or 60 men and their supporting equipment (engineers). Known as a Higgins boat, these vessels were the most effective of this that took part in those landings, weighing 52 tons, 13 metres long and capable of 9 knots driven by two engines. The craft needed a crew of four.

LCVP. A landing craft for 36 men and three tons of stores. 1 m. long, it weighed 18 tons. Its speed was nine knots and it had a crew of three.

LCA. This British-built landing craft was designed to carry 35 men and 800 kilos of equipment. Its all-up weight amounted to 13 tons and was 12 m. long. It was capable of 6 knots and was powered by two Ford V8 engines driving twin screws.

LCT (S). A larger American vessel designed to carry 5 Sherman tanks or 9 trucks or 150 tons of stores, 35 metres long and weighing all-up 268 tons. Capable of 7 knots, it was powered by 3 226 hp. Engines, driving 3 propellers and carried a crew of 13.

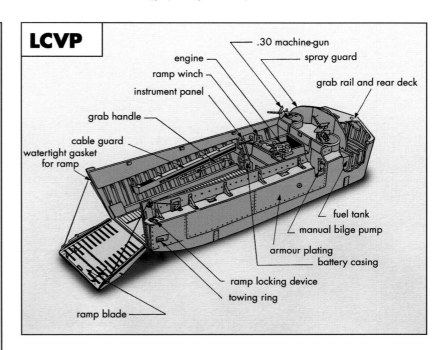

A LCVP is on view at the Omaha 6 June Museum. Here one can see the shape of the bow designed to break the force of the waves.

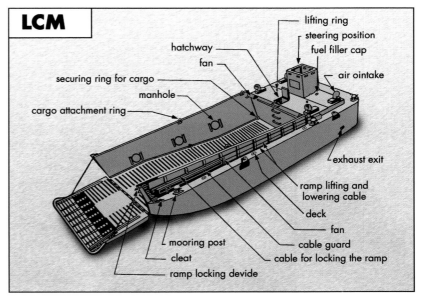

Here, elements of the 1st Infantry Division (as can be seen by the divisional insignia on the soldiers' blouses) are taking part in pre-embarkation exercises. GMC trucks are being reversed into an LST. (US Navy)

Here the men have been loaded into LCA's (Landing Craft Assault). For Operation Overlord, there were 486 such vessels available. With a length overall of some 12 metres, they could transport 35 men and 500 kg. of equipment, to land directly on a beach. (US Navy)

cans. Task Force O would be protected by sixty-four P-38 "Lightning" fighters flying top cover. In all, the Allied Expeditionary Air Force (AEAF) had 7,520 planes at its disposal.

Another important supporting element would be Joint Assault Signal Company (JASCO) personnel to assist in communications between the beach and the Navy ships. They included nine Naval Shore Fire Control Parties (NSFCP), an Air Liaison Section with thirteen Air Liaison Parties (ALP), and a Beach communications section. Communication and coordination of naval fire support would be critical to success.

The assault on Omaha Beach into Sectors Dog, Easy, and Fox was set for H-Hour, 0630. This would be one hour after low tide and just after sunrise at 0558. These were the conditions the planners of Overlord felt were necessary for success and only available on 5, 6, and 7 June 1944. If these dates did not work, the invasion would have to be postponed, awaiting similar conditions, which would not occur until July. Landing at the lowest possible tide was critical to the engineer effort to open lanes through the obstacle belts. This also would allow the tank battalions to assault the beaches at H-Hour a good distance from the German strong points with sufficient light to engage any that remained after the air and naval bombardment. Following almost immediately would be the first assault wave, eight companies of infantry plussed up to an average of two hundred each for the landings. More than two thousand Americans were set to land at H-Hour.

The Overlord strategy directed the two Regimental Combat Teams to land on Omaha Beach with one battalion size organization each, four companies, in the three initial waves. Their landings would be preceded by aerial bombardment at 0530 followed by a naval bombardment at 0600. Each RCT would be supported by an armor battalion of thirty-two Duplex Drive, or DD, tanks scheduled to land just ahead of them. There would

This view shows tanks loaded onto a LCT. They are not amphibious DD type but have been fully waterproofed to enable them to be offloaded into one metre of water without drowning the engine.(US Navy)

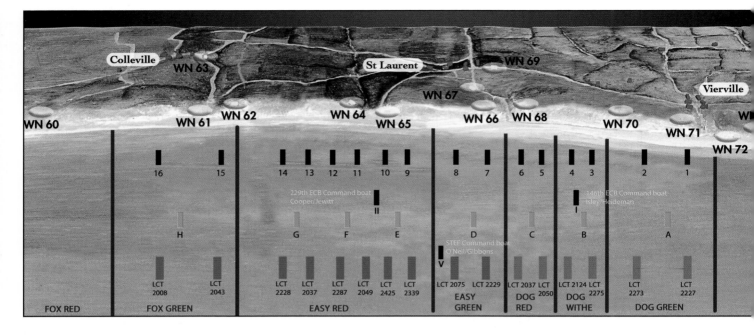

Colleville WN 63 St Laurent WN 69 Vierville

WN 67

WN 60 WN 61 WN 62 WN 64 WN 65 WN 66 WN 68 WN 70 WN 71 WN 72

16 15 14 13 12 11 10 9 8 7 6 5 4 3 2 1

229th ECB Command boat Cooper/Jewitt 146th ECB Command boat Isley/Heideman

II I

H G F E D C B A

STEF Command boat O'Neil/Gibbons

V

LCT LCT LCT LCT LCT LCT LCT LCT LCT LCT LCT LCT LCT LCT LCT LCT LCT LCT
2008 2043 2228 2037 2287 2049 2425 2339 2075 2229 2037 2050 2124 2275 2273 2227

EASY DOG DOG
GREEN RED WITHE

FOX RED FOX GREEN EASY RED DOG GREEN

Special Engineer Task Force - Teams 1-6 were responsible for lanes in the "Dog" Beaches, 7-14 the "Easy Beaches" and 15-16 the "Fox" beaches. They would be followed at H+08 by Gap Support Teams A, B, and C in Dog, D-G in Easy, and H in Fox.

also be engineers to open critical lanes through the German obstacles for follow-on waves. This would allow for a continuous flow of supporting units throughout the day, beginning with artillery and heavy engineers.

The RCTs landing in the first wave each had the additional support of a field artillery and engineer battalion, plus a medical battalion. They would be followed by a second wave at 0700 and a third at 0730. In addition to the infantry, each of the assault waves included headquarters elements, supplies and equipment, and specialists to enhance the success of the assault. There would be antiaircraft battalions to protect the landings from the Luftwaffe, navy personnel to manage the beach and assist in offloading, and medical personnel to help treat the wounded. After the first waves had secured the beachhead and opened lanes through the obstacles, there would be a continuous flow of men and equipment directly onto the beach. Almost immediately, the construction of an artificial harbor would begin just off Omaha Beach. With no natural port available, two "Mulberry's," built in English ports, would be floated across the Channel and into place. They would be the key to supplying the Allied forces as they advance through Normandy and beyond. Mulberry "A" would be constructed in the Bay of the Seine just off Omaha Beach.

Critical to the success of the initial landings were the tanks of the 741st Tank Battalion, supporting the landings of the 16th RCT and the 743rd Tank Battalion with the 116th RCT. Each battalion was comprised of thirty-two Duplex Drive (DD) Sherman tanks outfitted with canvas skirts to allow them to float. They were to be dropped off 6,000 yards from the beach and use their two propellers to push them through the Channel waters at a speed of 5 knots and onto Omaha Beach. The experimental configuration had been tested numerous times during practice landings in England and performed well. Once on the beach, the tanks would engage any remaining German bunkers or hardened positions while protecting the infantry advance. Well in advance of D-Day, Allied commando teams had frequented Omaha

Beach to map obstacles and provide geologists samples of the sand, to insure tracked vehicles would be able to move across the beach.

A Special Engineer Task Force (SETF), under the command of Lieutenant Colonel J. T. O'Neill, comprised of sixteen teams of the Army-Navy demolition experts, was set to land just before H-Hour. They included the 146th Engineer Combat Battalion (ECB) landing in "Dog", with the 116th and the 299 ECB in "Easy", along side the 16th RCT. Each team generally consisted of a Gap Assault Team (GAT) of Army engineers to destroy the obstacles on the land and a Naval Combat Demolition Unit (NCDU) to deal with any underwater obstacles. The assignment of each team was identical; open a lane fifty yards wide to allow the follow-on landing boats of infantry and supporting units and equipment to reach the area behind the well-placed German beach obstacles. Teams 1-6 were responsible for lanes in the "Dog" Beaches, 7-14 the "Easy Beaches" and 15-16 the "Fox" beaches. They would be followed at H+08 by Gap Support Teams A, B, and C in Dog, D-G in Easy, and H in Fox.

As the tide rose, the second and third waves would pass through these gaps and at high tide, boats would be able to unload their cargo of men and materials right at the seawall. Heavy engineers would arrive with Tank dozers from the Company A from each of the Tank Battalions. They would fill tank traps and open vehicle lanes from the beach and through the draws to begin the advance inland. Heavy Engineers would then begin building airplane runways to allow for critical supplies to be brought in and wounded to be returned to hospitals in England to receive the best possible care.

The follow-on waves on D-Day would include critical pieces of artillery. The 5th, 7th, 32nd and 33rd Artillery Battalions would land in support of the 1st Division, while the 110th, 111th, 224th, and 227th Artillery Battalions would arrive in the 29th Division sector. There would be M-7 self-propelled tank destroyers from the 62nd Armored Field Artillery (AFA) Battalion that would support the 1st Division and the 58th AFA with the 29th Division.

Antiaircraft support included the 457th AAA Battalion on the Green and Fox Beaches and the 467th AAA Battalion landing in Sector Dog. There was even support from the 81st Chemical Battalion in case the defenders resorted to the use of gas. In addition, later waves would include landing boats carrying elements from Signal Battalions, Medical Battalions, Quartermaster and Ordinance Battalions.

The goal planners had set for Omaha Beach was for the 1st Infantry Division units to push south as fast as possible and reach the lateral road by the evening of D-Day. When the 29th Division units reached the coast road, they were to turn west toward Isigny. If the 2nd Rangers had reached Pointe-du-Hoc, the Twenty-Niners were to link with them and continue west. If the Ranger mission there had failed, the guns were to be destroyed before moving on to link with the 4th Division units at Isigny. It was an ambitious plan.

The Defense of the Golden Beach

Generalfeldmarschall, Field Marshall, Erwin Rommel had been appointed as the Inspector General of German coastal defenses in October 1943, and was quick to recognize Normandy's "golden beach" as a possible Allied landing objective. During a visit to the beach defenses in May he told the defenders, *"I know the British from France in 1940 and from north Africa. They will land at the very place where we least expect them. It might be here."* The slight crescent curve to the beach reminded him of the bay in Salerno where the Americans had landed in Italy. Whether it would be *Tommies*, slang for the English, or *Amis*, Americans, he was convinced any assault against the Atlantic Wall must be stopped on the beach. The defensive plan would place as much firepower as possible forward, leaving only a notional reserve. "They must be stopped on the beach and driven back into the water," he concluded. He was also convinced any assault would come at high tide and that holding the beach defenses, the Main Line of Resistance (MLR), was the key to victory.

To implement his strategy, each of the five draws of "the golden beach" was established as a *Stützpunkt*, or strong point assigned to a company-sized unit. Each of these positions contained at least one embedded resistance nest, *Widerstandnester*, or WN, smaller strong points manned by at least a platoon. German planners mapping the WNs used circles, resulted in them being compared to "a string of pearls" dotting the curving beach. Each was ringed with a perimeter of concertina wire surrounded by a minefield, and most possessed the equivalent firepower of an artillery battery. They had interlocking or cross fires with other positions, which meant in addition to being fired on from the front, any one or any thing landing on the beach would also be engaged from their flanks. The German positions were well camouflaged and their enfilading fire protected from frontal observation. The indirect fires were also well planned with aiming stakes on the beach to let the gunners know when to fire on any approaching enemy. Each kill box, or site for concentrated indirect fire, was indentified by the name of a German woman. "Dora," for example, targeted the low tide line.

There were fifteen *Widerstandnester*, starting with WN 60 in the east and stretching west to WN 74,

Tobruk for Machine-gun near the beach, on WN61. (G. Bernage.)

Two Tobruks on WN62, the first for Mortar and the other for MG. (E. Groult/Heimdal.)

Tobruk for Machine Gun on WN60. (D.Ashe.)

WN 61

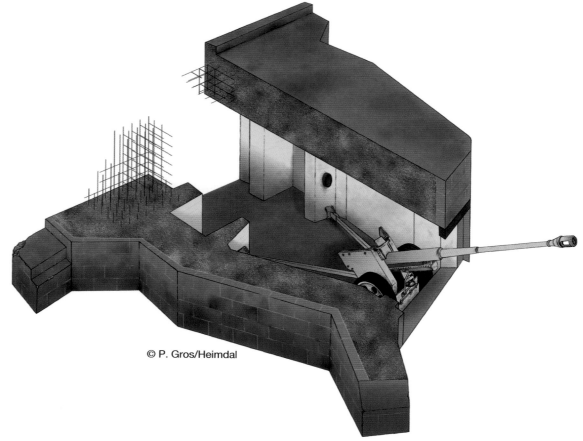

© P. Gros/Heimdal

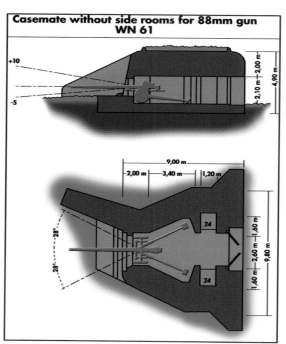

Casemate without side rooms for 88mm gun WN 61

WN 61

3. Casemate H 677, WN 61 (Heimdal).

4. WN 61 : Details of the rear of the casemate with the 88mm Pak 43/41 partly outside – the gun was knocked out at 0710 hrs in 6 June. (NA)

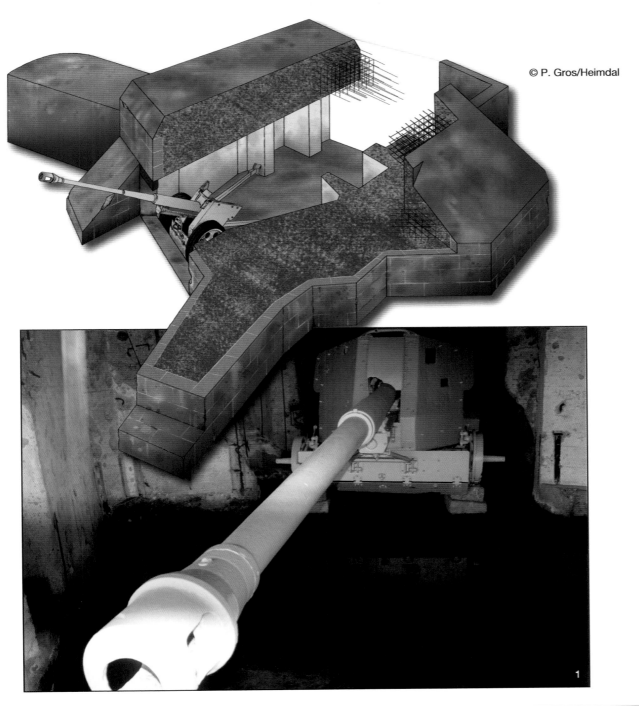

WN 72

1. The Type H677 casemate housed an 88mm gun which is preserved inside. This 8.8cm Pak 43/41 was an extremely powerful piece with a maximum range of 15,000 m. There were two guns of the same type on the beach, the other one being at WN 61 (G. Bernage).

2. This casemate photographed by the Americans in June 1944 still has its protective concrete side wall to shelter the gun from shells fired from out to sea, and on the left, the remains of anti-tank wall blocking off the entrance to the valley, after it was demolished. Where the wall joins the casemate a machine-gun embrasure can be seen. Note also the embryonic camouflage in natural stone (DAVA/Heimdal).

protected the expanse of Omaha Beach. They contained a total of thirty-five casemates some of which were still under construction on D-Day. The concrete casemates were the centerpieces of the German defenses on Omaha Beach. Constructed with 2 meter thick walls, they could only be

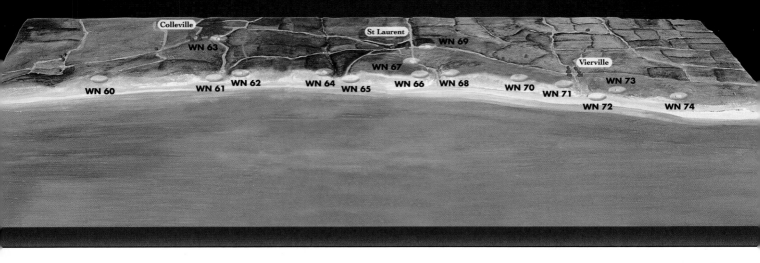

The German defenses. (Heimdal). Opposite: WN72 with the type H677 casemate, now suporting the National Guard monument. On the right: the casemate with two embrasures. (G. Bernage.)

Tank Turret on Omaha Beach. (NA.)

penetrated by naval guns from the battleships. Each housed a variety of weapons from large cannon to machineguns, and provided cover for command and control elements as well as forward observers. Their sides and roofs were often covered with dirt with camouflage netting used to cover any exposed concrete. Some were even disguised as homes to prevent detection from the Bay of the Seine. The casemates were constructed by Organization Todt which had gained recognition as the builder of the German autobahns. Its founder, Fritz Todt, was Adolf Hitler's Minister of Armaments. He was killed in a plane crash in 1942, but the effective work of his company was continued by his successor, Albert Speer.

There were two German Pak 43 direct fire howitzers on Omaha Beach, one encased in WN 61 and one in WN 72. These 3.5 inch anti-tank guns were better known by their caliber, 88mm. Manufactured by Krupp, Rheinmetall, these were clearly the most dangerous guns defending Omaha Beach. The armor plating of the American Sherman tank provided little protection against the high velocity sixteen pound shell fired from an 88. Situated on wheels and close to the ground, they had an effective range of 4,400 yards and easily covered every inch of Omaha Beach. Positioned four miles apart, they were housed in H677 concrete casemates. The guns were positioned in embrasures facing each other parallel to the shoreline and capable of providing enfilading fire from one end of the beach to the other. The flash from the barrels was protected by a concrete wall or wing on the waterside.

The defenses of Omaha Beach also included eight encased 75mm guns strategically emplaced in the WNs protecting the exits from the beach. Considered old and second rate, they were French or Czech guns captured during Hitler's advance through Europe. These weapons lined the Atlantic Wall since the eastern front opposing the Russians had priority for the newest and best German equipment. These guns were housed in H612 casemates similar to the H677, but smaller. There were also eighteen 50mm antitank guns housed in reduced size H677-type casemates. The defenses also included six Nebelwerfer mortar pits, thirty-eight rocket batteries, and numerous Tobruk positions. Tobruks were concrete bunkers flush to the ground, housing a variety of machineguns and the *Panzerstellung* or tank turrets, often from captured or destroyed armor such as the French Renault tank. Tobruk positions also concealed deadly German mortars from observation. In the Wehrmacht trenches built atop the cliffs and along the beach were eighty-five machinegun positions and inland, four artillery batteries. In all there were 167 German defensive positions on Omaha Beach; forty-four percent were in hardened, bombproof enclosures.

The German Navy, or Kriegsmarine was responsible for defeating any Allied ships that appeared in the Channel. They utilized 105-152 mm destroyer-size guns, intended to be "battleships in the dunes." There were three of these heavy batteries, which could influence the landings on Omaha Beach. The first consisted of the four 155mm guns of Battery 4/HKAA1260 manned by the Kriegsmarine and located to the east on the cliffs of Longues-sur-mer. The second was Battery 2/HKAA1261 to the west on Pointe-du-Hoc, with four mobile 155 guns manned by the army. Battery 3/1/HKAA1261 consisted of four 122 mm exposed guns manned by the army and located on Utah Beach at St. Martin-de-Varreville. Each site included forward observation bunkers with surveillance radars to direct the fire from the battery.

Between the Vierville Draw and St. Laurent over a mile to the east, was a dirt road where soldiers, uniformed personnel known as *"Hiwis,"* and local French workers had constructed rows of barbed wire interlaced with mines and deep tank ditches. *Hiwi* came from the German word *"Hilfswillinger"* meaning "willing to help." In lieu of going into a prison camp, often captives from the eastern front were offered the opportunity to serve in the German Army. The most trusted were given the opportunity to actually serve in Wehrmacht units, but most became drivers, cooks, messengers, etc.

The German defenders of Omaha Beach also included *Volksdeutsche,* German peoples from across Western Europe, such as Poland and even parts of Russia. The war had taken its toll on German manpower and Hiwis and Volksdeutsche were necessary to fill the declining ranks of static or lower priority units, particularly along the Atlantic Wall. Also there were the *Fedgendarmeries,* Wehrmacht military police constantly patrolling the roads. German soldiers called them *Kettenhunds,* or "chained dogs" trained and ordered to shoot anyone trying to escape to the rear in violation of the *Führerbefehl.* This was Adolph Hitler's decree that each defensive position be held to the last man. Extremely hated by the German soldiers, they could easily be identified by the gorget that hung from their neck.

The local French citizens were generally left undisturbed by the Germans occupying the area around Omaha Beach. Their homes were often used to house soldiers considered in garrison or allowed to have time away from the defenses. Many of the French were hired to support the construction of obstacles. A few of the farmers provided trucks for the effort along with horses and wagons. The French detested the presence of the Germans, but generally accepted the reality of their occupation and worked to get along with them. The efforts of the French Resistance, *Maquis,* however, are an entirely different story.

A significant natural feature found on Omaha Beach was the stone embankment below the seawall. Channel high tides had built this bank of stones known as "shingle." Following D-Day American Engineers used these stones for the foundation of the roads they would construct inland toward Paris. As a result, until recently, the stones were no longer found on Omaha Beach, but now they are washing ashore below the cliffs on both ends of the beach. As the Americans landed they tried to bury themselves in the stone embankment for protection against the murderous direct fire they faced from the German guns, but mortar and artillery rounds landing in the piles made it very dangerous to pause here.

A variety of German obstacles, placed only a yard apart in most places, stretched beyond the line of shingle. At low tide there was an expanse of 400 yards of open beach. The defenders expected the invasion at high tide, so the obstacle belt was heaviest near the embankment. Obstacles were positioned to rip the bottom out of the landing craft, tip them over, or blow them up. There were over 1,000 iron hedgehogs, *Tschechenigels,* brought from the defenses of Czechoslovakia and

A significant natural feature found on Omaha Beach was the stone embankment below the seawall. Channel high tides had built this bank of stones known as « Shingle ». (David Ashe.)

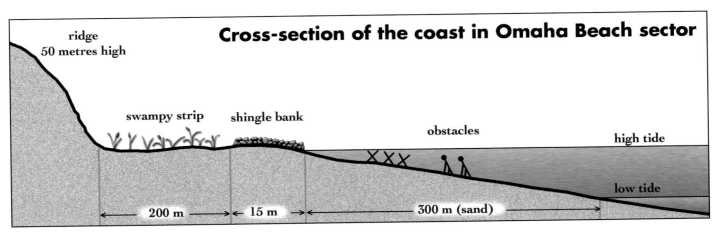

Cross-section of the coast in the Omaha Beach sector. A ridge some 50 metres high with a more or less steep slope dominated the shoreline consisting of a swampy strip liable to flooding and a wide beach of fine sand. The shingle bank at the top of the beach was quite prominent. (Heimdal)

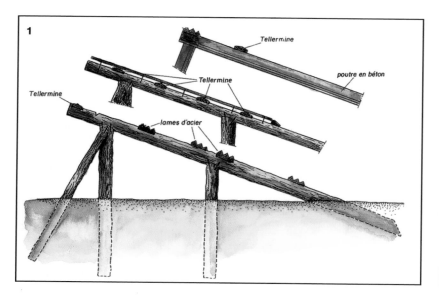

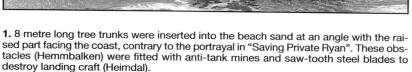

1. 8 metre long tree trunks were inserted into the beach sand at an angle with the raised part facing the coast, contrary to the portrayal in "Saving Private Ryan". These obstacles (Hemmbalken) were fitted with anti-tank mines and saw-tooth steel blades to destroy landing craft (Heimdal)

2. This is how the beach appeared shortly after the landings. The tree trunks, which came from the Forest de Cerisy were transported to the beach by requisitioned farm carts, but on the evening of 5 June the work was far from complete and the obstacles had only been installed at the top of the beach (Bundesarchiv)

3. A Czech Hedgehog preserved outside the Omaha 6 June museum at St-Laurent. (Heimdal)

4. The two types of Czech Hedgehog (Heimdal)

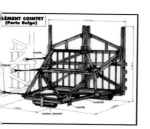

Belgian Gate. (Heimdal.)

similar looking concrete Tetrahedrons, pyramid shaped obstacles topped with *Tellerminen,* mines. In addition, eleven thousand mines had been placed on the beach, in the lanes leading to the cliffs and on the high ground above. These dense minefields were covered by machineguns, primarily MG42s capable of firing up to 1,500 rounds per minute. They could create an impenetrable wall of lead, especially when interlocked with a similar position resulting in crossfire.

There were 200 Belgian Gates, large steel obstacles set in concrete. Identified as "C" elements from their name "Cointet," they were of French design and originally in the Maginot Line where they were used to block roads and trails. There were 2,000 wooden stakes, *Holzpfaeles,* buried in the sand, with mines atop every third one. A line of 450 tree trunks, *Hemmbalkens,* elevated at one end on a bipod and then sloping toward the Channel were positioned to flip any landing craft passing over it. To expedite the construction of the wooden obstacles, the Germans used high pressure hoses from a fire department in Bayeux to open deep holes in the wet sand in less than three minutes. Previously, using pile drivers took almost an hour to dig a hole deep enough to sink the log obstacles.

Hidden just beyond the low tide line were mines and antisubmarine nets hidden in the Channel waters. Further out at sea was a well-placed system of mines creating a danger to the shipping lanes. The once feared German air force, the *Luftwaffe,* had been practically destroyed in the Allied effort to set the conditions necessary for suc-

2 The Assault

1. View from the embrasure of the casemate for the 75mm machine gun of the WN73, there was a dominant view, over the WN72, on all the beach below towards east. (David Ashe.)

2. German painting kept inside the bunker, which reproduces the same landscape towards the east. (David Ashe.)

3. And another one reproducing the landscape towards the west… (David Ashe.)

4. Double embrasure casemate for 50 mm gun on WN72. Here we see the embrasure facing west, towards « La Pointe de la Percée ». The other one, which was facing east to cover the beach, is now walled and can be distinguished in the background. (David Ashe.)

WN71

WN71 - The observation post.

WN 71 dominates the entrance to "D-1"", the valley entrance leading to Vierville-sur-mer (see pages 26,27 and 29). On the edge of the plateau, an observation post (**3** on plan p.26) with two openings offering an exceptional view to both the west and east.

1. Entrance staircase of the observation post, perfectly preserved. It stands on private land, making these photos so interesting!

2. Panoramic view looking west from the observation post.

3. An exceptional view of the entire beach as far as WN60...

4. Like WN73, the terrain is painted on the eastern half of the observation post. Note also the impact of a shell.

5. Detail of the painting allowing the Germans to adjust target priority.

6. Remnants of the wooden framing in a recess.

7. The access corridor with recess.

(Photos Theodore Shuey)

This painting released on the 50th Anniversary of D-Day depicts the chaos on the beach that morning. Renowned Artist James Dietz captures the struggle of American soldiers as they advanced through the obstacles of Omaha Beach. Titled « 29 Let's Go ! » and commissioned by American Art & Antiques Inc., the scene represents the determined effort of all the men landing on the « Golden Beach ».

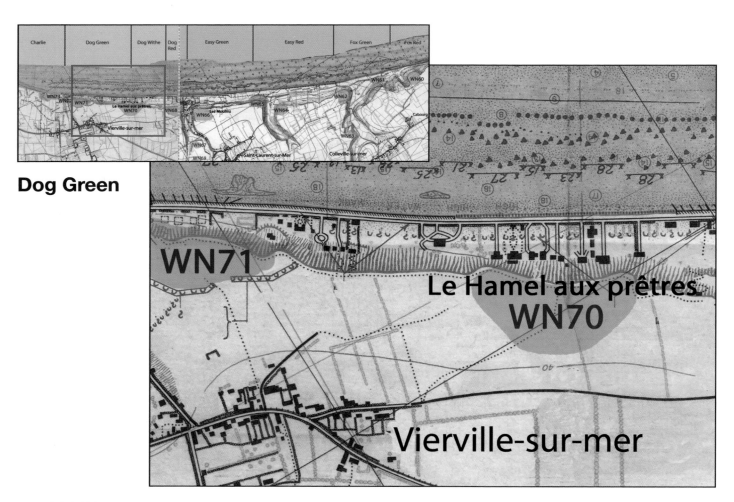

Dog Green

WN71

Le Hamel aux prêtres
WN70

Vierville-sur-mer

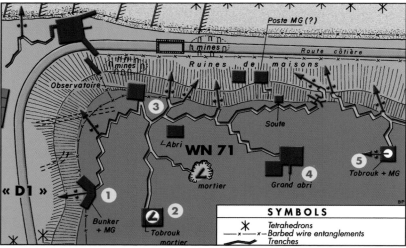

Poste MG (?)

Route côtière

Ruines de maisons

mines

mines

Observatoire

« D1 »

1

Bunker + MG

2

Tobrouk mortier

3

Abri

WN 71

Soute

mortier

4

Grand abri

5

Tobrouk + MG

SYMBOLS

Tetrahedrons
Barbed wire entanglements
Trenches

1. Casemate for 2 machine-guns. **2.** Tobruk for mortar (and picture opposite). **3.** Trenches and observation post. **4.** Big shelter. **5.** Tobruk for machine-gun. (Heimdal.)

Opposite: tobruk for mortar (**2** on the map).

Right: casemate, **1** on the map.

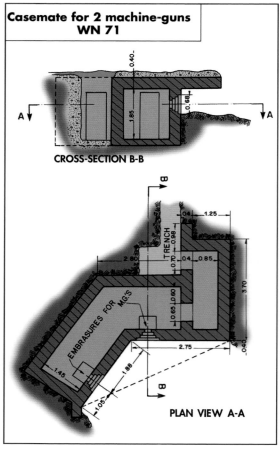

Casemate for 2 machine-guns WN 71

CROSS-SECTION B-B

TRENCH

EMBRASURES FOR MG'S

PLAN VIEW A-A

1. This view taken from the sea shows the entrance to the valley leading to Vierville (on the right) and the wide beach, the only sector where a coastal road existed in 1944, which the Americans called the "sea wall". One can see the location of WN71 overlooking the entrance to the valley and below on the beach the two casemates on WN 72. (Heimdal)

2. Photo taken shortly after the war facing westwards showing the two WN 72 casemates, the embrasures of which could dominate the beach.

Dog Green

The Dog beach sector identified by the color "Green" was 970 yards wide and included the Vierville Draw, exit D-1. This was the most critical landing site since it included the only hard surface road leading from the beach inland. Recognizing its value, if the Allies chose to assault the beaches on the Norman coast, the German planners had created four WNs in a classic strongpoint to defend against any landings in this sector.

East of Dog Green were the cliffs of Pointe de la Percee and WN 74 with a perfect view of the entire stretch of Omaha Beach. It had been the site of two giant Würzburg and one smaller Freya radar positions, but all three had been destroyed by bombing attacks prior to D-Day. The position still had two very dangerous 75mm guns facing east and covering most of sector Omaha. It also held an antiaircraft gun and multiple machinegun positions. WN 74 was defended by elements of the 11/726 Grenadier Company and with a command post overlooking the beach as far east as the cliffs below St. Honorine des Pertes.

Moving along the top of the cliffs to the east was a trench line which protected the defenders from observation from the beach below. It had multiple machinegun positions as it stretched east to a second defensive site, WN 73. The Allies identified this site as "the fortified house." Its defenses centered around a summer beach house built in a small depression in the cliff line with elements of 11/726 Grenadier Company. It housed twelve machinegun positions with two in casemates. There were also three Tobruk mortars, and the site housed another important observation bunker.

The cliff trench line running further east led to WN 72. There were multiple encased machinegun positions here with a casemate housing a 75mm gun which covered the beach to the east. Inside the D-1 draw also facing east was a machinegun embrasure built into the cliff. Below on the beach was another double embrasure with a 50mm antitank gun and multiple machineguns. A second antitank gun was positioned on a ring stand above. All of the positions were connected with a zigzag trench line with multiple sniper positions protected by wire obstacles and mines. Elements of 11/726 manned the very strong WN 72.

The D-1 draw was blocked by an eight foot high concrete wall with an opening through overlapping walls to allow passage of individuals. Beyond the wall the beach road was cut by a large anti-

Model illustrating the state of WN 72 shortly before the landings. On the left is the 88mm casemate in front of which were the remains of the Hotel Legallois, left there for camouflage. On the right in the foreground is the double embrasure casemate.. On 6 June 1944 there was still work to be completed. (Model by – Sud Modélisme)

Aerial view of the Vierville sector where A/116th and the 2nd Ranger Battalion suffered such heavy losses. One can see the emplacements of WN71 up on the high ground at the entrance to the valley. The village of Vierville is in the background. (Photo Romeo India).

tank ditch. On the beach side of the wall was a Type H677 casemate disguised as a beach house housing the 88mm Pak 43 howitzer. It was under the first floor of the Hotel Legallois destroyed by the Germans to open up the fields of fire for WNs 74, 73, and 72. On the opposite side of the wall the ground rises sharply and near the top was another observation bunker with two Tobruk mortar positions and multiple machinegun sites in the trench line leading east. Inside the draw in the cliff was a machinegun embrasure directly opposite the identical position in WN72. Together they could provide a deadly crossfire on anything entering the draw.

The German defenders of D-1 were called to their defensive positions in the early morning hours of June 6. The first sightings of the Allied fleet were reported at 0502. When the firing from the Allied naval bombardment ended at 0624 Hours on D-Day they began emerging from the safety of their bunkers. Though very unsettled, they found their positions only minimally damaged from the Allied Naval attack. It was time to "lock and load" their deadly weapons that had been carefully concealed and zeroed in to repel any assault onto the beach. Each position had detailed range maps painted on the wall, identifying terrain features or obstacles within their sights. The sketches inside the casemates provided the range or distance each gunner needed to effectively engage the assault force on or as it approached the beach. From snipers to artillery, the German defenders knew when to initiate their fires to achieve maximum effect.

As the morning light began to rise in the east, the gunners could begin to see the outline of the Allied flotilla at sea. Soon they could make out the outline of landing boats carrying Company A, 1st Battalion, 116th Infantry Regiment of the 29th Division as they emerged on the horizon. They were

headed for the Sector "Dog Green" and draw D-1 leading to the community of Vierville. Overlord planners had sought a force ratio of 4:1, four Americans landing against one German defender. In reality though, after landing, Company A, even with tank and engineer support, would be facing superior numbers, a ration closer to 1:4, of defenders positioned on the beach and high ground defending Dog Green. In an attempt to help the odds, the entire 1st Battalion of the 116th RCT was to land here, one right after another on D-Day. Company A would arrive in the first wave at 0630, followed in twenty-minute intervals by Company B, then Company C, and finally Company D. Dog Green was the objective of the entire 1st Battalion, 116th RCT, commanded by Lieutenant Colonel John Metcalfe.

Company A crossed the line of departure aboard six British LCAs with armor plating to provide as much protection as possible from German direct fire. The additional weight of the iron sheets, however, coupled with choppy waters, caused the boats to begin taking on water. The soldiers initially enjoyed the luxury of being seated on wooden benches, but soon found themselves standing and desperately using their helmets to bail the rising water around their feet.

The tremendous load being carried by the soldiers onboard compounded the heavy weight of the armor plating on the LCAs. Each man was burdened with a minimum of sixty pounds, more frequently one hundred pounds, of weapons, ammunition, and equipment. Less than a mile from the beach, one of the Company A boats, LCA 911, possibly damaged while being lowered from the deck of its transport, the Empire Javelin, took on water so fast that it quickly sank leaving the soldiers floating in the icy cold Channel. The men struggled to escape their heavy loads while activating the tubes of their CO_2 life belts. Fortunately only one man, Private James Padley, the radio operator, was lost. Some of the men proposed trying to swim to shore, but 1LT Edward Gearing, their platoon leader, cautioned against it. "We can't make it. It's too far. We'll wait and get picked up by some passing boat." For the next four hours the men would bob in the rough Bay of the Seine before finally being picked up by one of the returning landing craft.

The five remaining LCAs continued to the beach, unable to stop and assist. The orders to British Sub Lieutenant Jimmie Green, wave commander of the British Navy 551 Assault Group in LCA 910, were perfectly clear. He was to stop for nothing until he delivered Captain Taylor Fellers and his Company A onto the beach in front of the Vierville, D-1 draw. Stopping for nothing, he recalled, "We were to go as far in as we could and drop the ramp on the sand."

Before landing, Green was shocked to observe the beach was "flat as a pancake." The Air Force bombing had completely failed in its mission of striking the German positions on Omaha Beach and creating holes in the sand to protect the landing soldiers. In the thick cloud cover, afraid of hitting the landing fleet below them, the concerned bombardiers had delayed their drop from five to thirty seconds to avoid friendly casualties. This pause was long enough for their bombs to land harmlessly in the farm fields well south of Omaha Beach. It would be 1000 Hours before the cloud cover lifted enough to allow the Allied air armada to provide effective air support for the landings.

Captain Fellers' boat landed first, and he had his men exit and lie down on the wet sand before turning to bid Coxswain Green goodbye. There was an eerie calm as the LCA backed out. It was 0636 hours. Navy Lieutenant Joe Smith, the Beach Master for D-1, landed nearby and recalled, "The Germans let us alone on the beach. We didn't know why, we could see the Germans up there looking down on us, it was a weird feeling. We were right in front of a German 88 gun emplacement, but fortunately for us they were set to cover down the beach and not toward the sea, so they could not see us."

The Vierville Draw was a classic German strong point. It was covered not only by the casemates in WN 71 and 72, but also ranged easily by the guns of WN 70 further east, plus WNs 73 and 74 to the west in Sector Charlie. It could also be covered by positions in the east like the 88mm gun casemate of WN 61 almost four miles away.

Suddenly, all Hell broke lose. The German *Feldwebels*, Non Commissioned Officers, gave the order *"Feuer,"* fire! Immediately the gunners positioned on the cliffs above Objectives Charlie and Dog Green opened up on Company A with everything they had. Almost immediately a well-placed mortar struck the last Company A boat landing before it could even drop its ramp. The resulting explosion and murderous fire immediately caused Captain Fellers to shout to his men to get up and follow him in a race across the remaining three hundred yards of open beach. He was quickly cut down by machinegun fire. It was all over in a matter of minutes. Four surviving boatloads of 116th RCT infantry were no match for the defenses in four German WNs. With no other targets in sight, for some time the German gunners scanned the

beach for any survivors. Company A would essentially cease to exist as a fighting unit.

The engineers landing moments later ran into the same murderous fire. Lieutenant Wesley Ross of the 146th Engineers recalled, "We were under heavy small arms fire almost immediately, and machine guns, mostly unseen by me, were tracking our movements." The surviving engineers would do what they could, but were unable to open any lanes in Dog Green. Follow on assault waves additionally would have to make their way through the German obstacle belt as the fast rising Channel tide moved across the western landing sites on Omaha Beach.

The plan was for the DD tanks of Company C, 743rd Armored Battalion, commanded by Lieutenant Colonel John Upham, Jr., to arrive in Dog Green just before H-Hour to support the assault companies of the 116th RCT. Their landing plan was changed at the last minute though, as a result of the rough seas. Navy Lieutenant Dean Rockwell, commanding LCT (Landing Craft Tank) Group 35, decided to deposit the DD tanks directly onto the beach. "It was apparent that the sea would not be ideal for launching the tanks," he recalled. Landing at 0630, the company of sixteen M4 Sherman tanks immediately drew heavy fire from the 75mm and 88mm guns defending the Vierville Draw. Four tanks were hit immediately, and three LCTs were struck while offloading their critical cargo.

Miraculously, a few members of Company A, 116th RCT survived by hiding in the rising surf as the

First Lieutenant Ray Nance, A Company, 116th RCT, Dog Green. (116th Foundation.)

Captain Ettore Zappacosta, Company A Commander, 116th RCT. (116th Foundation.)

Pfc Gill Murdock, A/116th RCT, Dog Green. (116th Foundation.)

Captain Zappacosta was hit and killed almost immediately. (Coll. R. Sales.)

tide washed the bodies of the killed and wounded toward the beach. Private First Class Dom Bart remembered, "I floated around in the water for about one hour and was more dead than alive." Along the edge of the rising surf the bodies rolled back and forth like logs. The Company A men who had radios or heavy equipment strapped to them stayed where they fell as the tide rushed inland. Most of their bodies would never be recovered. Wounded Private Thomas Valance of Company A recalled, "The bodies of the other guys washed ashore, and I was one live body amongst many of my friends who were dead and, in many cases, blown to pieces." Any sign of life immediately drew fire from the snipers or machine gunners that had gotten their first taste of combat.

After twenty minutes, right on schedule a second group of boats appeared directly in front of D-1. It was the second wave of the 1st Battalion, which was comprised of Company B and the Company A Executive Officer, 1LT Ray Nance, landing with more men and support equipment. As he jumped into the rising surf, he quickly realized what had happened to his company. "I turned around and saw the bodies in the water—they were bumping against one another it was so thick. There was nobody in sight. I was hit three times before I got to the high-water mark."

Company B, 116th Infantry, leading the second wave into Dog Green, arrived in LCVPs just right of where Company A had basically been annihilated. The coxswain of the command boat quickly recognized what was occurring on the beach in front of D-1 and began turning his landing craft east to find a safer position to offload the soldiers. "We can't go in there. We can't see the landmarks. We must pull off," he shouted. In response, Captain Ettore Zappacosta the Company B commander pulled his .45 pistol and ordered, "Take this boat straight in." The result was similar to what had occurred with Company A, as the German gunners shifted their fire to the four arriving Company B boats. As the ramp drops on the lead boat, CPT Zappacosta is hit and killed almost immediately.

It was a standing order in the 29th Division that the leaders were to be the first off of the boats. This was a costly decision, which left the soldiers of the 116th initially leaderless in their early hours on Omaha Beach. CPTs Fellers and Zappacosta, dozens of Lieutenants and senior NCOs were the first ones killed as they tried to lead their men forward. One of the survivors of Company A, PFC Gil Murdock recalled hiding in the surf and looking for someone to tell him what he should do. Finally, he recalled, "I saw somebody crawling quickly back towards us, and I saw it was George Roach with the flamethrower. I asked what had happened and he said all of the officers were dead, and all of the noncoms were dead, and he and I, as PFCs, were the senior men on the beach as far as he could see."

There were Company B survivors also, as 1LT Leo Pingenot and SSG Odell Padgett landed and quickly lead their platoon across the beach to the safety of the cliffs to the west. On the way, two survivors of Company A joined them as they raced for the base of the heights. The tide was now reaching the obstacle belt, so the Company B men who remained on the beach were able to hide in the rising surf or behind the wreckage of tanks and vehicles destroyed in front of D-1. Still, there was little they could do other than struggle to survive as the murderous fire from the machine guns and snipers on the cliffs above them continued to pour down. Meanwhile, British Sub-Lieutenant T. E. Arlidge in charge of the remaining Company B boats elected to turn east to seek a safer landing site. The officers on board in charge of these LCAs were First Lieutenant William Williams, now the ranking officer in Company B and First Lieutenant Walter Taylor.

Sergeant Robert Sales of Company B, 116th RCT who proceeded to land in Dog Green recalled,

Colonel Charles D.W. Canham, commanding 116th Infantry Regiment. (US Army.)

Sergeant Robert Sales, B/116th RCT. (116th Foundation.)

Lieutenant Colonel John A. Metcalfe, 1/116th. (US Army.)

"When I looked across there to the beach, I saw nothing but tracer ammunition from machine guns everywhere. No men were in front of us, the ones that had landed in front of us were already dead, and they were in the water." Lieutenant Colonel Metcalfe, commanding the 1st Battalion's Company A, B, C, and D, arrived in the midst of the chaos with four boats of his headquarters element. Landing in column, the Germans were able to engage the boats one by one as their ramps drop. Lieutenant Colonel Metcalfe led the survivors across the beach to the seawall where he was pinned down just to the right of where his first two companies have landed. His Executive Officer Major Tom Dallas observed the scene, "They made it because the man ahead caught the bullet which might have felled them and so saved them from the fire." Metcalfe was without any means of communication and unable to either describe the disaster to his superiors or to change the landing plan. Pinned down, all he could do was watch the chaos until finally being able to leave the safety of the embankment in the afternoon.

Company C was next to land in Dog Green, but its commander, Captain Berthier Hawks, assessed the destruction there and wisely allowed his coxswain to seek a better location for their landings. Captain Walter Schilling, commanding Company D in the last assault wave of the 1st Battalion did not follow Company C and plowed straight into the disaster. Corporal Donald Fisher remembered that as the ramp of his landing boat opened, Captain Schilling was killed immediately. "Instead of going off the lowered end gate, we decided it was safer to go over the sides and that is how we got onto Omaha Beach. There were bodies and wounded all over the beach and in the water." For the next hour, the survivors of Company D were caught in the rising tide while they struggled to reach the beach below the cliffs.

Making his way in, another member of Company D, Sergeant Robert Slaughter, who would one day

1. Sergeant Robert Slaughter D/116th RCT, Dog Green. (116th Foundation.)

2. Staff Sergeant Bob Slaughther, somewhere in Germany, 1945.

provide the impetus for the American National D-Day Memorial in Bedford, Virginia, recalled, "There were dead men floating in the water and there were live men acting dead, letting the tide take them in." Upon reaching the shingle embankment after over an hour in the water, the surviving members of Company D were able to rest for a short time. Then suddenly the 116th RCT commander, Colonel Canham, approaches them yelling, "Get the hell off this damn beach and go kill some Germans." Despite visible wounds to his wrist and arm, the Colonel continued moving up and down the beach, providing much needed leadership and encouragement.

The battleship Texas was built at Newport News and launched on 18 May 1912, taking part on the blockade of Vera Cruz in 1914. Modernized between the wars, this elderly ship participated in the Torch landings in North Africa in November 1942 after which she escorted convoys in the Atlantic up until April 1944. Her next assignment was to support duties for the landings on Omaha beach, flying the flag of. Rear Admiral Carleton F Bryant, commanding the Force O Bombardment Group **(1)**. On 6 June 1944 at 0550 hrs. the Texas opened fire on the Pointe du Hoc and later, used her firepower to open up the beach Exit at Vierville. Her powerful armament consisted of 10 365mm guns, 16 127mm and 40 40mm which had an important role to play during the landings. She later supported the landings in Provence and on Okinawa. Decommissioned in 1948 she is now anchored at Houston where she serves as a state memorial. **(2)**

Of the engineer teams, numbered 1-6, assigned to open a lane on the Dog Beaches, only one had been successful, and it was further east. This meant there was very little place for follow on craft to land in Dog, and soon the rising tide began concealing the German obstacle belt. At 0830, the commander of the 7th Naval Beach Battalion (NBB), Commander L. C. Leevers, responsible for the landings in Omaha Beach east, called a halt to future attempts until the engineers could clear more lanes. Omaha Beach was a cluttered mess.

Observing the interruption of the landings, the German observation post on Pointe de la Percee made the following report to *Oberstleutnant*, Lieutenant Colonel Fritz Ziegelmann the Assistant Chief of Staff of the 352nd Infantry Division in Trevieres: "At the water's edge at low tide near St. Laurent and Vierville the enemy is in search of cover behind the coastal zone obstacles. A great many motor vehicles-and among these ten tanks—stand burning at the beach. The obstacle demolition squads have given up their activity. Debarkation from the landing boats has ceased; the boats keep further seawards. The fire of our strongpoints and artillery was well placed and has inflicted considerable casualties upon the enemy. A great many wounded and dead lie on the beach." This positive report would affect the counterattack plans to drive the *Amis* back into the sea.

Clearly, the landings by the 116th RCT into Dog Green had been a disaster. Historian Ronald J. Drez described the scene perfectly when he wrote, "Still the boats of the 116th Regiment came on like moths drawn to a flame. Their reward for their perfect navigation to the correct landing beach was to enter into the jaws of hell." Its entire 1st Battalion had essentially become combat ineffective until replacement soldiers and cross leveling of Regimental leadership allowed it to rejoin the fight as it moved into the farm country or *Bocage* of Normandy.

The D-1, Vierville Draw would be under constant Naval bombardment the rest of the morning. It would remain closed though, until noon when firing from the USS Texas and several destroyers silenced the remaining resistance, allowing a force from nearby Dog White to advance down the paved road and open the critical draw from the rear. The few remaining German defenders quickly surrendered, allowing Engineers of the 121st Engineer Battalion to reach the wall blockading the draw. Sergeant Noel Dube of Company C, who did much of the work recalled, "We finally reached the wall at around 1315 hrs. and found 20 boxes of explosives in the trailers of two bulldozers and our expert John Olenek, spread them out on the wall. He broke open one of the boxes, inserted a detonator and unrolled an electric wire. We got the men under cover and when John pushed the button, a ball of fire erupted, throwing lumps of concrete and stones all over the place, but when the smoke dissipated, the two walls were down." Lieutenant Colonel Robert Ploger, commanding the battalion remembered, "I was astonished by how completely the wall was destroyed. It turned out that the Germans had not reinforced the wall with steel rods. That was a fatal mistake." In no time dozers cleared the remaining debris. D-1 was open just after 1500.

Today, driving down the famous D-1 Vierville Draw Avenue de Bedford, you are looking at the beach of Dog Green. Note the double machinegun embrasure in the cliff to your right or the east as you near the bottom. On the evening of D-Day the 29th Division established its headquarters in the remains of a stone quarry located just below. You pass memorials to the 5th Engineer Group, the 29th Division, and the American Rangers. At the end of the draw is the National Guard Memorial to its "citizen soldiers" who sacrificed so much on D-Day. It rests atop the casemate still housing the German 88mm cannon of WN 71 that was very effective during the first hour of the landings.

The concrete wall that blocked the draw stretched from here across the road to the stone retaining wall on the opposite side which displays a plaque to the 29th Division Engineers. In the steep hillside above the wall were multiple machinegun positions and an observation bunker. Looking west, during low tide you can see a portion of the ruins of Mulberry A. It is a short but worthwhile climb to the 75mm gun casemate on WN 72. The cut housing the ruins of the fortified house in Objective Charlie can be found four hundred yards in the cliffs above the beach to the west.

Sector Charlie

Landing to the right of the 116th RCTs Company A and B, at 0656 in Sector "Charlie" were LCAs 418 and 1038 carrying "Task Force B", comprised of Rangers from Company C, 2nd Ranger Battalion, commanded by Captain Goranson. They landed in the extreme eastern portion of the cliffs designated as Sector "Charlie," that stretched 2,320 yards from the Vierville Draw west beyond Pointe du Hoc. Having received no news from Lieutenant Colonel Rudder, the Task Force mission at this point was to follow and support the 116th's attack through the Vierville Draw. Then, reaching the coast road they would follow it to Pointe du Hoc. If the attack to open the D-1 was unsuccessful, their orders were to assault the cliffs to the west and destroy Stützpunkt le Guay, WN 74. This would allow them to proceed the three miles necessary to attack Pointe du Hoc from land and reach any survivors of the 2nd Ranger Battalion's Task Force A.

The cliffs in Sector Charlie were part of WN 74, defended by 11/726 Grenadier Company. Their defenses began at Pointe de la Percee in the west and ran east to the fortified house in WN 73. Positioned on the destroyed radar site on the Point were two 75mm guns which had a perfect view of the entire expanse of Omaha Beach. There was a trench line zigzagging along the top of the cliffs with multiple sniper and machinegun positions.

As the two boats carrying Captain Goranson's Ranger force landed, LCA 418 immediately took multiple hits from German mortar and artillery fire. The survivors and the Rangers in LCA 1038 ran

WN71 - The casemate for two machine-guns is still dominating the entrance (D1) of the Vierville draw. See page 26. (G. Bernage.)

across the open beach, as direct fire from the defenders was shifted from the Company A and B survivors to the Rangers. Of the 68 Rangers under Goranson, 19 were killed in the landing and crossing. In a matter of minutes, the survivors made it across the beach to the bottom of the 100-foot cliffs and out of direct firing range of the murderous German gun positions above. One of the experienced Rangers noted at every one hundred yards there were different colored crossed poles on the beach. "Mortar Markers," no doubt there were locations of preset fires for the gunners above. This planning allowed the Germans to zero in very quickly on the American assault force all across Omaha Beach.

Privates Jake Shefer and Thomas Lovejoy, survivors from Company A, 116th RCT, saw the Rangers advancing and gladly joined them. In addition, twenty members of Company B, 116th RCT, that were pinned on the beach by the continuing murderous German fire, made their way to the Rangers. These would be the only members of the five Company A and four Company B boats that landed in front of D-1, to get into the fight on D-Day.

As the Germans continued to fire at anything showing signs of life in front of the Vierville Draw, CPT Goranson led his group of survivors along the base of the cliffs protecting WN 73. Lacking grappling hooks or climbing equipment, he tasked Ranger First Lieutenant William Moody to find a crevice or opening where he could scale the 100-foot heights, using his knife, bayonet, and American ingenuity. Taking Ranger Sergeants Richard Garett and Julius Belcher, along with PFC Otto Stephens, Moody slipped undetected west along the base of the cliffs looking for a place to begin his assent. As Goranson waited, the Germans in the trenches above dropped their potato mashers (hand grenades) on the Rangers. They even had ropes holding unexploded bombs suspended from the top of the cliffs, which when cut allowed them to fall on the men trapped below.

Sergeant Moody, Ranger Battalion.

Suspended from the top of the Cliffs. (NA.)

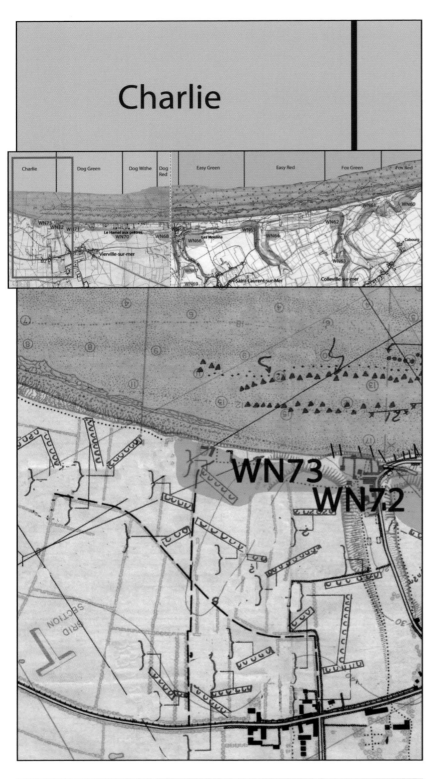

Charlie

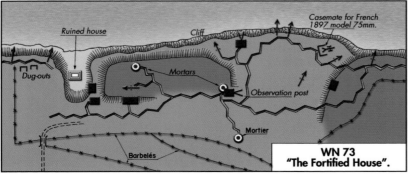

WN 73
"The Fortified House".

In what probably seemed like forever, but in reality only a few minutes, Moody found the best site and sent Private Stephens climbing up, using his bayonet to pull himself higher and higher. Once on top, he secured a rope to a pole the Germans had dug into the ground to support a ring of barbed wire and dropped a piece of rope for Moody. The Lieutenant signaled Captain Goranson and the remaining Rangers began climbing. Once on top, he took the ten-foot sections of toggle rope each man was carrying and sent a long piece down to the others for their climb. By 0730, all of his Rangers and the few survivors from Company A and B of the 116th RCT had reached the top and began their attack toward the fortified house. They destroyed a machine gun position still firing on the beach, then a mortar section. Along the way Lieutenant Moody was killed, and First Lieutenant Sid Salomon, the 2nd Platoon Leader, took charge.

The ensuing fight took seven hours as the Rangers moved through the German trench system taking out one position after another. When the struggle ended, sixty-nine Germans had been killed while many escaped inland. With most of WN 72 and all of WN 73 destroyed, at 1430 Goranson headed off with a patrol to attack WN 74 at Pointe de la Percee. When he neared the position, he could see that the big guns there had been destroyed; one had even fallen onto the beach below. The USS McCook was credited with destroying the position at 0948. The guns had been very effective firing on the American landing boats and tanks on the Dog beaches to the east. What remained, however, in WN 74 were well-hidden Wehrmacht defenders determined to prevent the surviving Company C Rangers from advancing to Pointe du Hoc. There was a lot to overcome before continuing further west. Captain Goranson was the basis for Tom Hank's character, Captain John Miller, in the movie, *Saving Private Ryan*.

The wounded German survivors from WN 72, 73, and 74 sought help in the homes at Gruchy and along the coast road. Later they would be joined by American wounded and treated by 29th Division Medics. Local citizens still relate stories of German and American wounded, suffering side by side, in their homes on the evening of D-Day and beyond.

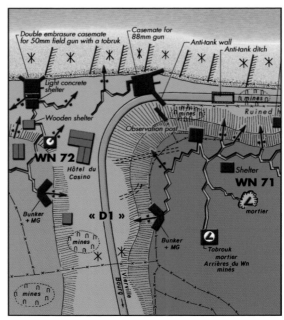

WN73 was well placed to the west of the beach, perched on top of the cliffs which commenced here.

Ghost-like remains of a ruined house, silent witnesses to the fighting in 1944. This villa housed the men of the Kriegsmarine (German Navy).

Portions of Sector Charlie are still visible. WN 74 can be reached from the coast road by turning onto the small road leading north at the Chateau d'Englesqueville, just before the red water pump housed in the stone enclosure. Drive as far as you can, then walk to the cliffs and turn right to follow the trench line to the site of WN 74 and the ruins of the German radar site still visible.

WN 73 and the fortified house can be found by turning north at the Musee d'Omaha Beach and driving toward the campground. As the hard surface road turns to the right, stay straight, taking the dirt road with the fence on the right. When the fence ends, park and follow the path to the cliffs and the remnants of the house and WN 73.

WN 72 is west of the Vierville Draw, above and behind the Hotel du Casino. Looking west to the high ground you will see the casemate for the 75mm cannon, which had a devastating effect on the beach to your right. Walk to the casemate and turning around, view the length of Omaha Beach. To your left are steps which led to additional German positions inside the campground. The outline of the German trench system can be seen to the west behind the casemate. Returning to the beach, note the shingle bank on your left as you walk to the double embrasure that housed a 50mm cannon and two machineguns. The ring stand atop the embrasure is still visible.

One can see the casemate for the French 75mm field gun-see also pages 21 and 25. (Photos Heimdal.)

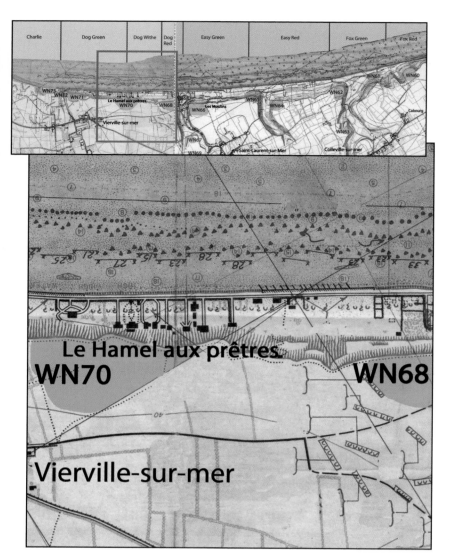

Le Hamel aux prêtres

WN70

WN68

Vierville-sur-mer

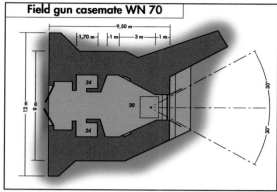

Field gun casemate WN 70

Dog White
WN 70

Dog White

The second Dog sector was assigned the color "White." It was the 700 yard stretch of beach located directly in front of WN 70 and the cluster of beach houses known as Hamel Au Pretre. The German defenses here were centered on the cliffs, with a path connecting to positions to the beach. WN 70 included two Tobruk mortar positions, two 75mm cannon, one of which was encased, a 20mm antiaircraft position, and four machineguns in Tobruks along the zigzag trench works at the edge of the cliffs. Elements of the 11/726 Grenadiers were here connected to 8/916 Grenadier Company defending further east. There were few Germans positioned on the beach when the American landings began in front of WN 71 to the west and WN 68 to the east. Strangely, few

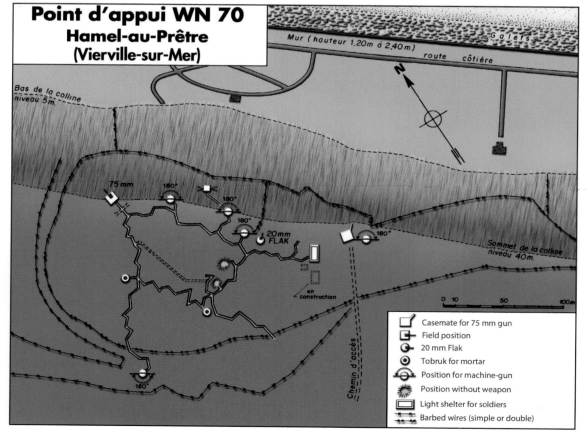

Point d'appui WN 70
Hamel-au-Prêtre
(Vierville-sur-Mer)

Mur (hauteur 1,20m à 2,40 m)
route côtière
Galets

Bas de la colline
niveau 5m

75 mm
20mm FLAK
en construction

Sommet de la colline
niveau 40m

Chemin d'accès

⬦	Casemate for 75 mm gun
⊞	Field position
◔	20 mm Flak
⊙	Tobruk for mortar
⌓	Position for machine-gun
✴	Position without weapon
▭	Light shelter for soldiers
▦	Barbed wires (simple or double)

landing craft approached WN 70, so the defenders located there began engaging the assault into Charlie and Dog Green.

Company G, of the 2nd Battalion, 116th RCT was to land in the first wave at the same time as Company A, but to their left, or east, in Dog White. This supporting attack should have drawn some of the German fire coming from WN 70, 71, and 72 at H-Hour. The Company G boats, however, got caught in the strong easterly current from the shoreline eighteen-knot northwest wind and were swept further east into Dog Red. This left the Dog White sector vacant of any serious infantry landings for the first hour following H-Hour, but later supporting units did begin to arrive here on schedule.

Navy Lieutenant Rockwell's decision to land the tanks he was responsible for was clearly the correct one. He later recalled that "At 0505, this command contacted Captain Ned Elder via tank radio, and we were in perfect accord that the LCTs carrying the 743rd Battalion would not launch, but put the tanks directly on the designated beaches." When the LCTs touched the sand of Dog White, however, the Company C tanks landing here suffered the same fate as those landing in Dog Green, only worse. They were offloaded just to the east of the most dangerous German weapon on the beach, the 88mm, Pak 43 howitzer in WN 71. The tanks driving onto the beach also did not go unnoticed to the 75mm and 50mm guns hidden in the cliffs throughout the other *Widerstandnester* protecting Omaha Beach. Only six of the sixteen survived the landings on the Dog Beaches.

Staying just ahead of the rising tide, the M-4 Shermans began returning fire on the German casemates, only to find their 75mm cannon could do little damage to their thick walls. It would take naval gunfire to eliminate the positions. Fortunately, offshore, naval observers were becoming keenly aware of the problem. In no time, the destroyer USS McCook went into action. A young nineteen year old Corporal William Preston of Company C, 743rd Tank Battalion recalled what happened next. "Whenever any of us fired a burst of tracer at a target, the destroyers, standing in so close they were almost ashore, fired a shot immediately after us each time hitting what we were firing at on the nose first shot." Soon the dangerous 88mm gun in WN 71 was neutralized. It was 0720.

Gap Assault Team (GAT) 1 from the SETF, caught in the strong easterly current, landed here in Dog White instead of Dog Green. They immediately drew deadly fire from WN 70 which included the houses of Hamel Au Pretre. Despite the heavy German mortar and machine gun fire, GAT 1 was able to open a gap 50 yards wide. This allowed the surviving tanks to work their way toward the seawall where they began to engage the encased positions, which had inflicted so much damage on the first wave. The gap would also provide an opening for the landings of follow-on waves, particularly the critical command and support boats set to land here. This, the only gap opened in the Dog landing area of the 116th RCT, would contribute significantly to the later success of the infantry reaching the high ground above Omaha Beach.

The two Company B, 116th RCT boats that diverted their planned landing in Dog Green came ashore in Dog White between WN 68 and 70. First Lieutenant Taylor and his men landed in the "breakwaters," which extended into the sand west

of WN 70. Their arrival was partially concealed by the smoke from grass set afire by the naval bombardment. It filtered along the base of the cliff as he led his men to the top of the high ground. Soon, Captain Berthier Hawks and the seven boats of Company C in the third wave at 0720 landed here, also avoiding the disaster in Dog Green. Finally, there was a company-sized organization landing in Dog White.

Covered somewhat by the continuing smoke from grassfires and German guns, Company C landed without incident, allowing Hawks to lead his men to the seawall at the end of the beach. He recalled, "We landed with 194 men and officers, and I estimate that we lost about 20 in crossing the beach. Atop the seawall were rows of barbed wire to prevent Company C from crossing the beach road and reaching the base of the cliffs." Sergeant John Polyniak remembered, "Our boat team made it to the seawall with no casualties. We hardly hesitated when we reached the wall. I was carrying a Bangalore torpedo, and I reached over the wall, placed it under the enemy wire, and blew it with my igniter." This was one of several openings cut in the wire obstacles, which allowed elements of the 116th RCT to cross the beach road and reach the base of the cliffs.

Landing at 0730 in Dog White, right behind Company C and between elements of Company's B, F, and G, came the Dog Sector command group for the landings. It included Brigadier General Cota and elements of the 29th Division Headquarters and Colonel Charles Canham Commanding the 116th Infantry Regiment. They arrived aboard LCVP 71, which reached the sand after several attempts to maneuver through the obstacle belt west of WN 68. First Lieutenant Jack Shea, General Cota's aide, noted, "The first cover available was the partial screen provided by a DD tank of C Company, 743rd Tank Battalion, which had landed at H-6. There were 18 of these tanks standing just above the water line on Dog beach."

Brig-Gen. Norman Cota, deputy commander of the 29th Inf. Div.

The command group would make their way to the seawall, where General Cota led them through a gap in the wire above. He directed the infantry to continue up the cliffs, while he turned east to the Les Moulins Draw to check on the 116th RCT's 2nd Battalion. He also wanted to linkup with his counterpart, Brigadier General Willard Wyman and the 1st Division Headquarters. Colonel Canham, wounded in the hand as they reached the beach, would proceed west toward the Vierville Draw to get the 1st Battalion survivors moving. The mix of 116th RCT soldiers now had the leadership they had needed to begin to breakout.

Larger landing craft, LCIs, were beginning to approach the beach at Dog White. These boats carried mainly support units of MPs, Engineers, and medical personnel. At 0740, the stern and midship of LCI 92 was hit and burst into flames. LCI 91, trying to make its way through the obstacle belt, was also hit and caught fire when a round struck a soldier carrying a flamethrower. LCI 94, attempting to land was hit by artillery fire, but was able to withdraw from the beach as the tide rose. LCIs 91 and 92 remained on the beach throughout the day, consumed in flames. Although the Charlie and Dog beaches were covered with destroyed boats and tanks, plus the bodies of hundreds of members of the 116th Regiment, a strong force was building on Dog White.

Along with the supporting LCIs, Lieutenant Colonel Max Schneider arrives at 0753 with Task Force C,

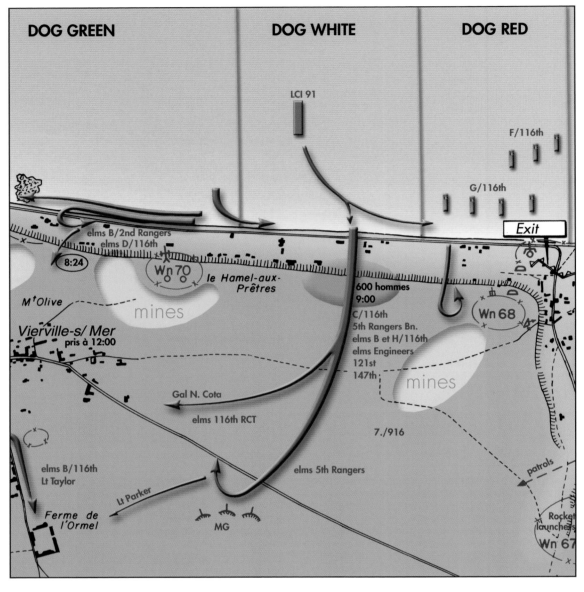

Starting out from Dog White, a considerable penetration onto the high ground was achieved towards Vierville. General Cota set up his headquarters at 0839 just below the summit. (Heimdal.)

Lieutenant-colonel Schneider, 2nd Ranger Battalion.

comprised of 650 Rangers from his 5th Ranger Battalion, along with Able and Baker Companies of the 2nd Ranger Battalion. The 2nd Battalion units landed to the east and immediately came under heavy fire from WN 70-74. With landings diminishing in Charlie and Dog Green, the German defenders now began concentrating their fires into Dog White. The large LCIs' waves were lucrative targets for the German defenders. Schneider's Rangers however, landed in LCAs and lost only six men as the Rangers raced across the beach to the seawall.

Safely there, General Cota met Schneider. "You men are Rangers!" He shouted. "I know you won't let me down. Colonel, you are going to have to lead the way. We are bogged down." After a brief discussion, Cota turned to the men around Schneider and uttered the famous words, "Rangers! Lead the Way!"

At 0830, the Rangers and the men of Company C of the 116th RCT constituted a strong enough force to begin ascending the cliffs diagonally to their right. They made their way carefully across the trench works they found on the high ground and through the German minefields behind. One

of the first to reach the top of the cliff, Captain George Whittington, commanding Company B of the 5th Rangers, found three Germans manning a machinegun nest. One of the *Jerries* jumped up shouting, *"Bitte, bitte,"* to which Whittington responded with a burst from his Tommy gun. Turning to Private Carl Weast nearby, he said, "I wonder what *bitte* means?"

Moving toward Vierville, the 5th Rangers met the surviving members of the 2nd Rangers who encountered difficult resistance on their way up to the top. The group organized and moved off to the west toward the village. Once there, the Rangers had orders to move west on the coast road toward Grandcamp to locate and assist Task Force A and Lieutenant Colonel Rudder at Pointe du Hoc. If that mission had failed, Schneider's men were to destroy the German position from the rear. The absence of any news from Rudder or his men was very unsettling to the Ranger force as it moved toward Vierville.

By 1000, General Cota had also reached the top of the cliffs in Dog White, turned west and rejoined the Rangers and men from Captain Hawk's Company C. Their advance greatly reduced the amount

Captain George Whittington.

of direct fire from the high ground onto this section of Omaha Beach, but the ongoing landings were still subject to deadly indirect fire. The group's move beyond Vierville was slowed by snipers and German machineguns using smokeless powder which made it difficult to identify their location. As the 5th Rangers moved through the town, headed west to reach Pointe du Hoc, they ran into stiff resistance. The delay allowed Colonel Canham to join them and reassess their next move. He ordered the Rangers to abandon any further attempt to advance west and prepare to defend Vierville from the expected German counterattack. Lieutenant Colonel Schneider protested the order, but to no avail and grudgingly followed it. Canham understood the Ranger's desire to try to reach Rudder and his men, only three miles away, but it was clear that holding Vierville was much more critical to the success of the beachhead.

General Cota was now focused on getting the Vierville Draw open. He moved back toward Dog Green and WN 72 at 1230, accompanied by his aide and a handful of infantry from the 116th RCT. The destroyers McCook and Thompson had been engaging the German positions there with support from the fourteen inch guns of battleship USS Texas. The firing had caused a number of the defenders to leave their positions and in no time fifty-four prisoners had been taken by the Americans. Cota slipped through the small opening in the wall at the base of the draw and ordered Engineers from the 121st Battalion that he found huddled on the other side to destroy the obstacle. The Vierville Draw and the village above were in American hands.

Lieutenant Jack Shea recalled what he saw as he followed the General onto the beach to locate the Engineers. "Bodies of riflemen, obviously of the 116th Infantry by the insignia they wore, were spread along the base of the concrete, inclined seawall. The first body lay about 40 yards east of the exit, and in any 100-yard sector from there down to Dog White beach there could be found

35 to 50 bodies." Cota now establishes the 29th Division Command Post in the draw and starts preparing for the German counterattack which he knows will be coming.

Lieutenant Taylor lost contact with the rest of the 116th RCT but continued to lead his group from Company B south. He crossed the coast road driving German defenders through the fields and hedgerows, taking fourteen prisoners. As he reached the crossroads just beyond the Ormel Farm he saw three truckloads of German soldiers, a part of the 7./916 GR counterattack, dismounting to advance toward Vierville and the D-1 Draw. Using slits in the walls surrounding the farm buildings, Taylor's small force engaged the Germans. Soon they were joined at the farm by a group of Rangers. Together they blunted the counterattack, but vastly outnumbered, Taylor decided he should withdraw and join the rest of his battalion approaching the coast road.

The Ranger force that came to his aide was led by Lieutenant Charles Parker. The group consisted of members of his 1st Platoon, Company A, that had also pushed south across the coast. Separated from the rest of the Rangers and unaware of the change to their original orders, Parker broke contact with the German counterattack force at 1430 and headed west toward Pointe du Hoc. The group crossed orchards and fields, taking forty German prisoners as they moved to their objective. They released the Germans in order to maintain the pace necessary to reach Pointe du Hoc before dark. At 2100, Parker along with twenty-three survivors of the difficult move, found Lieutenant Colonel Rudder's position. "Where the Hell is the rest of the fifth battalion," Rudder asked after welcoming the small group?"

"They must be right behind me," Parker replied. Neither man had any idea the Rangers were setting up defensive positions around Vierville. As night approached, Rudder had only eighty Rangers to hold the defensive perimeter around Pointe du Hoc.

US Navy

US Navy helmet with numerous coats of grey paint normally used for the maintenance of ships' hulls.

Helmet worn by the driver of a GMC amphibious DUKW ('Duck'). Note the painted, stylised duck.

LCVP (Higgins Boat) compass.

Engineer Special Force (ESB) 'Seahorse' insignia.

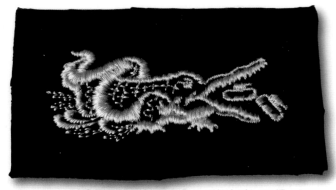

US Navy Amphibious Forces insignia.

1. 6th Naval Beach Battalion (NBB) helmet.

2. LCVP waterproof "floats." These floats served to help save boat crews in the water while waiting for the response of the Coast Guard.

3. Semaphore flags with their carrying case, naval instruction manual, US Navy helmet and US Navy Officer's peaked cap.

4. Semaphore flags training aid.

(Fonds Fantastic Attic/Bayeux.)

Dog Red

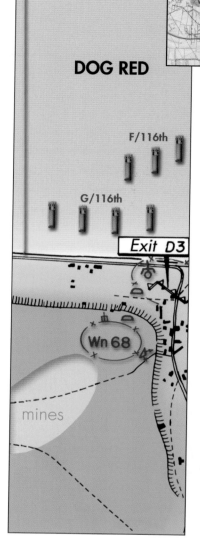

WN68 - the twin embrasure machine-gun casemate which controlled the Valley. (Heimdal.)

The Valley was blocked by a concrete antitank wall. (Coll. D. Tréfeu.)

Dog White today can be found centered between the D-1 Vierville draw and D-3 at Les Moulins. The villas in the Hamel au Pretre, destroyed by the Germans, have been replaced with numerous beach cottages. The Hardelay house, the large Normandy style home with the three foot stone wall and white picket fence on top, is near the base of the cliffs where the 116th and Rangers broke through. The outline of the zigzag path the Germans constructed leading from the beach to WN 70 can be seen on the hillside behind the home.

Dog Red

The stretch of Omaha Beach known as Dog "Red" included the D-3 or Les Moulins draw and the 480 yards of sand to the east. A small well-fortified beach house remained here, and it was the only stretch of beach that did not have Belgian Gates in its obstacle belt. A road used by the Germans to work on the defenses on the beach was next to the house and led straight inland to St. Laurent. An extensive tank ditch blocked the dirt road with partially prepared antitank positions on either end. Further up the road was an eight-foot high wall, blocking the route inland covered by machinegun embrasures located in the cliffs on either side. The

German defenses of WN 68 were positioned on the western side of the draw with two tank turret Tobruks and a 50mm encased cannon. On the cliffs above the draw was an extensive minefield covered by multiple machinegun positions. The defenses in these fields were part of the second line of defense. On the high ground facing the draw was a double embrasure machinegun position. Dog Red was defended by the 8/916th Grenadiers.

The first wave of landings in Dog Red consisted of four of the boats of Company G, 116th RCT that had been swept east from their planned landing site and three boats of Company F. Company G landed almost directly in front of WN 68 and the Les Moulins Draw, while Company F came ashore further east of the draw in front of WN 66. Both units were from the 2nd Battalion of the 116th RCT, commanded by Major Sidney Bingham. Private John Robertson of Company F recalled, "So here we are, all seasick, ahead of everyone else, no bomb craters to get in, and heading straight into machinegun fire. That was my definition of Hell."

The absence of the anticipated bomb craters gave the assaulting soldiers no place to avoid the murderous German fire. Major Thomas D. Howie, the S-3 or Operations Officer of the 116th RCT landing nearby, would write in an after action report, "It was the consensus of all officers and men questioned, that prior to H-Hour there was positively no evidence of friendly aerial bombardment of the beaches. There were no craters along the water's edge, no demolition of beach obstacles, and very little evidence of naval gunfire." Less than six weeks later, Howie would become immortalized as the "Major of St. Lo," killed commanding the 3rd Battalion, 116th RCT in its attack to liberate that city.

Sergeant John "Buddy" Thaxton of Company F and his mortar section survived crossing Dog Red, and he often wondered how they made it when so many others did not. "I guess with so many targets for them to choose from, they simply overlooked us." Still, the situation was nothing like that occurring in Dog Green. Partially obscured by smoke from fires set by the naval bombardment, many soldiers from the two companies were able to make their way safely through the beach obstacles and reach the shingle seawall at the end of the beach. Here the wire obstacles on top of the road above stopped them.

Some of the landing craft arriving in Dog Red got stuck on sand bars created by the runnels or deep cuts made by the strong easterly currents. This forced many soldiers to fall into deep water as they jumped off the lowered ramp. Salt water got into many weapons, preventing the soldiers from returning fire on the German positions. Second Lieutenant John White of Company G recalled, "We had our weapons covered by a plastic type bag during the run in, many of them failed to function on the beach and it was necessary to find cover behind an old wall and clean our weapons so they would fire. I remember thinking at the time that this was a heck of a time to be participating in a session on care and cleaning of the basic infantry weapon." The seawater was just another obstacle the Americans had to deal with on Omaha Beach.

Landing in the second wave here to avoid the murderous fire on Dog Green, the Company B, and 116th RCT boat of First Lieutenant William's platoon turned in near the base of WN 68. As it neared the dry sand, mortar rounds began to rain down on the boat. The men are able to exit the craft just before it was hit dead center by a round and blown

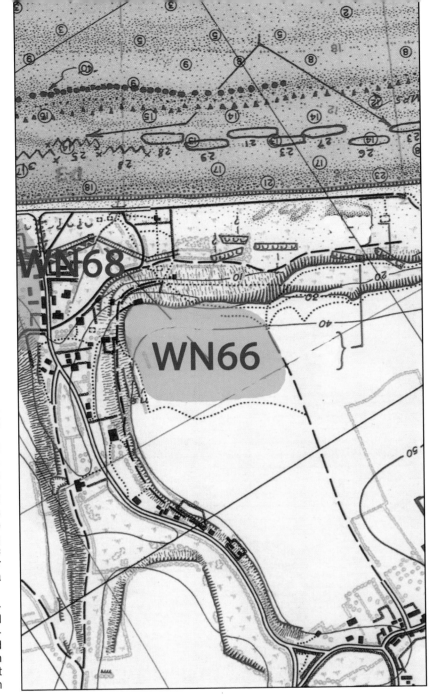

Major Sidney V. Bingham, Commander 2/116th RCT. (Heimdal.)

Private John Robertson (TSgt on the picture), F/116th RCT, Dog Red. (116th Foundation.)

First Lieutenant Williams, B/116th RCT, Dog Red. (116th Foundation.)

An aerial view of St-Laurent-sur-Mer taken on 2 December 1943 showing that work on the defences was not particularly advanced. One can see here the Moulins valley, future beach exit D3. WN 66 to the east of the valley was still only a rudimentary position. (coll. Museum Omaha 6 June)

apart killing the crew. Williams led his men through heavy fire and reaches the base of the high ground with only seven survivors.

Scanning the high ground above, Lieutenant Williams spotted an encased machine gun pouring murderous fire onto the beach behind him. Cautiously he leads his men in an attack to destroy the position. To avoid presenting a large target for the machinegun crew, he left his men and crawls toward the position, using high grass to cover his approach. Reaching hand grenade range, he pulled the pin and tossed the "pineapple" toward the embrasure. Unfortunately, it struck the concrete side of the opening and bounced back on him. He was wounded by shrapnel from the explosion and later by fragments from a German "potato masher," their wooden handle grenade, tossed at him. As he withdrew to join his men three rounds from the machinegun hit him.

Lying almost completely immobilized, Lieutenant Williams handed his compass and map to SSG Frank Price who came to attend to him and said, "It's your job now. But go the other way toward Vierville." Reluctantly, Price left the wounded officer and leads the group west, up and around the hill, away from WN 68. Williams would lie wounded until almost midnight when he was finally located and evacuated. Proceeding as directed, his men will link up with Lieutenant Taylor on the high

ground and proceed to Vierville. Including Taylor, Company B survivors here total only twenty-eight.

At 0720, the third wave of the 116th RCT, its 3rd Battalion, which was part of the regimental reserve, began landing in the rising tide amidst the breach obstacles. They had hoped to find open lanes onto the beach, created by the engineers in the earlier assault waves, but this was not the case. Lieutenant John T. Czuba, of Company I recalled the surprising scene. "Coming in small arms and machine gun fire crackled overhead and mortar and artillery fire burst around us. The ramp went down and I stepped off and I went, way over my head. I inflated my life belt and struggled about 50 yards to the beach." Pushing ahead, Company I would follow the route of Company G and scale the high ground to the area behind WN 68.

Private First Class John Amdondola of Company H recalled a terrifying incident he encountered as he landed. "Two of the men from my section got down behind a tetrahedron to escape bullets. An artillery shell hit the tetrahedron and drove the steel back into their bodies. I tried to pry the steel loose form the men but could not do it. Then I figured they were dead anyway." Nearby, when Private First Class Preston Bousman reached the base of the cliffs, he looked back at the beach behind him and saw nine landing craft. "Seven were ablaze and sinking," he recalled.

Company M follows next, and as Weapons Company, it brought in a number of support vehicles and ammunition. PFC George Fox was assigned as a driver of a halftrack loaded with 105mm ammunition for the guns of the 111th Field Artillery scheduled to land at 0900. Fox recalled his LCT circled offshore for a long time while the beach was closed before finally getting the order it was clear to land. "As the ramp dropped, I gunned the engine and the halftrack shot out and through deep water onto the beach. There, we were under fire immediately with machinegun bullets pinging off of the armor plate covering the windshield. The Lieutenant and I jumped out just before a round hit the vehicle completely destroying it. He was killed almost immediately. I ran for cover, picking up a BAR from a dead soldier, but was wounded almost immediately and laid on the beach until finally being evacuated the next day."

In the plan for the assault on Omaha Beach, the 116th RCT would have the support of another unit of the Virginia National Guard, the 111th Field Artillery Battalion. Their 105mm guns were to come in on DUKWs, but they were not able to stay afloat in the choppy Channel waters. Eleven of the twelve guns, their complete compliment of equipment, and 150 rounds of ammunition sank before reaching the beach. "To hell with our artillery mission. We've got to be infantrymen now," shouted Lieutenant Colonel Thornton Mullins, commanding the 111th, when he learned of the disaster. A short time later his determination would cost him his life, as he was hit by a sniper's bullet as he directed a tank in an attack on an enemy machine gun position the Les Moulins Draw.

At 0950, Rear Admiral Bryant, commanding the bombardment group, had seen enough. He radioed the destroyers, "Get on them, men! Get on them! They're raising hell with the men on the beach, and we can't have any more of that! We must stop it!" Moving to within 1,300 yards of the

A large russet-colored stone *Comite du Debarquement* monument marks the eastern boundary of Dog Red. (David Ashe.)

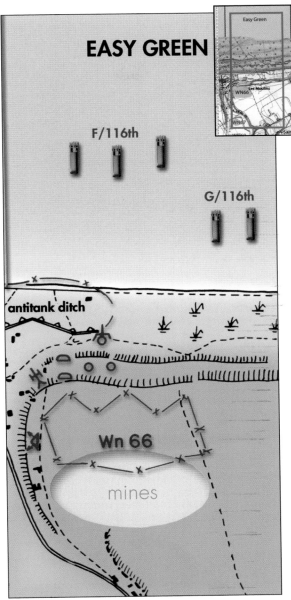

EASY GREEN

F/116th

G/116th

antitank ditch

Wn 66

mines

On board the battleship Augusta, Rear Admiral Alan G Kirk (left) and General Omar Bradley (2nd from left) observed the progress of operations on Omaha beach. Nothing went according to plan. (NA)

beach, the USS Carmick placed 5 inch gunfire into WN 66 and WN 68 to assist in opening the D-3 draw where so many infantrymen were pinned down. Observing the effective work of the destroyer group, in one of his next messages to General Bradley, General Gerow said, "Thank God for the Navy!" Rear Admiral Alan Kirk, in command of the entire Western Naval Task Force, supported the use of destroyers. "They had their bows on the bottom," he observed from the deck of his flagship the USS Augusta. They fired at point blank range throughout the morning and afternoon.

The dangerous Engineer effort to free the beach from obstacles continued throughout the day. "Taking advantage of the receding tide, about 8 or 10 of our demolition squad began slipping through the obstacles, hastily stringing wire in preparation for blasting open a passage through which landing craft might pass undamaged when the tide rose again later in the day. Just as they seemed to be finished and were grouped together fixing the fuse and detonator, a small shell came hurtling out of nowhere with precision-like accuracy and landed plump in their midst, sending their mingled bodies flying in all directions," recalled

The farm where the André family was living in June 1944. It was built on the slope leading up progressively to WN66 to which access was gained via the lane La Pissotière, seen here on the left running past the farm. Seen here is the main south facing façade looking toward the village of St. Laurent. During the night of 5/6 June the 11 German soldiers billeted at the farm left the building by the back door and out through the garden which was raised above the lane. They were all killed by daggers or strangulation by the American airborne troops and the body of the last one remained hanging over the garden which can be seen here facing the rear.

Seaman W. Garwood Bacon, 7th Naval Beach Battalion. Throughout the day, well-hidden German observers directed deadly indirect fire onto the entire expanse of Omaha Beach.

Today, at the bottom of the D-3 draw, a large russet-colored stone *Comite du Debarquement* monument marks the eastern boundary of Dog Red. Just to the west is a marker recognizing the failed British Commando Raid known as "Operation Aquatint" in August 1942. In the flat stretch of beach further west behind the existing houses, was the first American Cemetery after D-Day. The L'Omaha Restaurant sits atop a concrete base that once housed one of the Tobruk sites in WN 68. Today modern homes dot the hillside where well-positioned German machinegun nests covered the beach, but one pillbox near the top is still visible. To the left of the restaurant is "Rue du 116" which marks one of the routes the men of the 116th RCT used to reach the cliffs above and move into Vierville to the west.

Easy Green

The landing beach identified as Easy "Green" began in the Les Moulins Draw and stretched east 830 yards, almost halfway to Le Ruquet Draw. It's most notable position was the three-story house, which housed deadly machineguns positions below the ground level. It was located on the beach just below WN 66 and could provide enfilading fire across the center portion of Omaha Beach. Within the resistance nest defended by elements of the 8/916 Grenadiers were multiple machinegun positions. They covered the D-3 draw from the east with fields of fire on the beach in both directions. There were also two Tobruk heavy mortar positions and two Tobruk tank turrets. A 75mm cannon was positioned on the high ground in a partially constructed casemate, which was due to be completed on June 7.

During the early morning hours of June 6, two airborne drops occurred behind the beach near St. Laurent, one was unplanned and one planned. The unplanned drop consisted of a "stick," a load of paratroopers from the 101st Airborne Division, forced to bail out of their C-47 over land just before it crashed into the Bay of the Seine. It had been struck by German antiaircraft fire before reaching

its drop zone and turned back trying to reach its base in England. The crew quickly realized they could not make it and turned on the green light, alerting the airborne troops to jump before the plane descended further and reached water. At least a portion of these men were welcomed and hidden in the home of the Andre family in St. Laurent. During the early morning hours they killed eleven Germans attempting to leave a nearby French home to reach the WN 66.

The defense plan for the German soldiers defending Omaha Beach required fifty per cent of the defenders to be in their positions at all times. Each *Stützpunkt* had *Mannschafts* or personnel bunkers, concrete positions underground with bunks stacked three high. The quarters were tight, but allowed a place to rest as shift duty allowed. The other fifty per cent of the personnel were allowed to be "in garrison," *lagered* or billeted in French homes as nearby as possible. This group interacted with the civilians, buying eggs, milk, and butter when available, even paying to have their laundry done in the home. Essentially off duty, they were required to be prepared to return to the defense on short notice, normally through telephone lines connecting their quarters to the beach.

The second airborne drop was probably a well planned insertion of a commando team. General William Donovan, director of the American spy service during World War II, wanted agents working behind the German lines in France to provide intelligence on enemy movements. He created "Jedburgh" teams from the American Overseas Strategic Services (OSS), the predecessor of the Central Intelligence Agency (CIA), French Resistance, and MI6 personnel. Their mission was not only to gather information, but also to assist the local French Resistance in disrupting German attempts to reinforce their defenses on Omaha Beach. Although the specific mission of this team is unclear, they met and had coffee with a local, Gaston Dupont, before slipping into the darkness never to be seen again. Little is known of the success or failure of this group since its activity was classified as "Top Secret." Eighteen Jedburgh teams had been dropped behind enemy lines by June 14.

From the line of departure, Company E of the 116th RCT was to land in Sector "Easy Green," the D-3 draw to the east of the Les Moulins Draw. The strong Channel current, however, carried them a thousand yards east into the 16th RCT, 1st Division area. The only landings in Easy Green would be three boats of Company F, 2nd Battalion of the 116th RCT and two from its sister Company G that had also mislanded due to the strong current. To their front were WN 66 and the house on the beach with a strong German position covering the beach. Major Sidney Bingham commanding the 2nd Battalion, 116th RCT landed here and remembered,

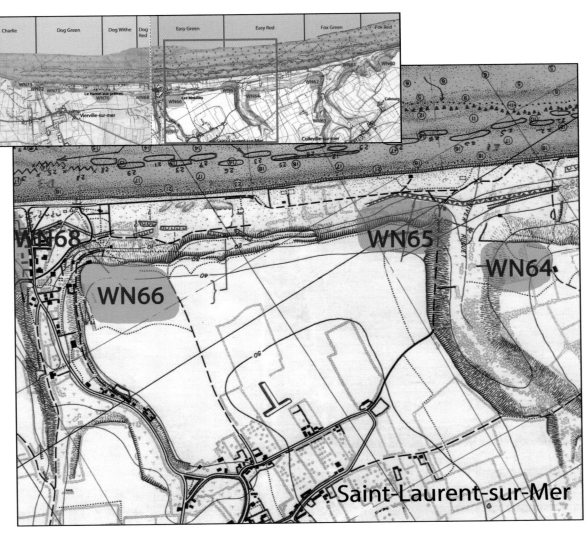

WN 66 extended over two levels and was an important position entirely surrounded by barbed wire, bordered by a minefield to the south while to the north ran lines of trenches along the edge of the slope. Firing positions were covered with logs. (NA).

Work was started on several casemates at the foot of the plateau but was never completed. Among these right at the exit of the valley from St. Laurent was an unfinished casemate **(1)** of which only the shuttering and reinforcing rods pointed skywards as at WN 64. Further to the right **(2)** was a double embrasure casemate which had not received its roof although it was camouflage painted to resemble a seaside villa; In front of it was an emplacement which was due to receive its tank turret on 5 June. (NA).

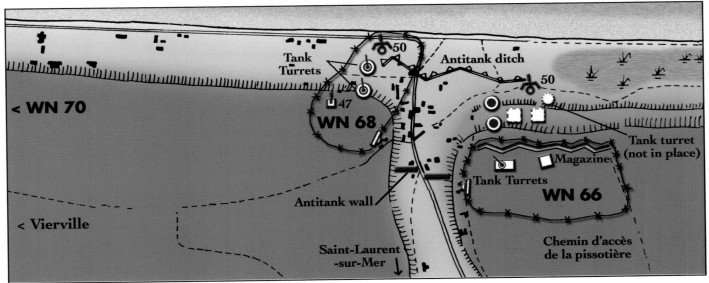

The « Bingham House », Easy Green. (NA/Heimdal.)

Sergeant Earl Wilkerson, HQ 3/116th RCT, Easy Green. (116th Foundation.)

"I finally crossed the beach and got to the shingle along the beach where about 100 men from F Company were seeking what little shelter that was afforded by the road. The only officer I could find was Lt Theodore Lamb, who was painfully wounded and very dazed."

Major Bingham proceeded to organize the soldiers he found to initiate an attack on the well defended structure, which would become known as the "Bingham House." It had a mansard roof with a tower and machinegun positions on the first floor. The house had repeatedly been hit by naval and tank fire, but still continued to pour hot lead into his 2nd Battalion landing craft from the ground floor. Helpless and frustrated, the young Major remembered, "An impression that overcame me at this juncture was one of complete futility. Here I was, the battalion commander, unable for the most part to influence the situation or do what I knew had to be done."

Using wire cutters, the men he organized cut an opening in the wire on the road above the shingle bank where the group had assembled. Soon fifty infantrymen were attacking the house. Quickly though, the soldiers of his 2nd Battalion realized none of their weapons would fire. As the tide rose, later waves of the units landing across Omaha Beach would be dropped in the rising water, which fouled their weapons and much of their equipment. Heavy items, especially radios, had to be dropped to allow the soldiers to swim or float onto the beach. Frozen under the continuing German fire, most of the members of Bingham's Battalion remained flat against the shingle, forced to clean their weapons before advancing any further.

A frustrated Bingham maneuvered alone toward the back of the house. Finally arriving safely in the rear of the structure, he met a group of engineers who had just destroyed the German gun from the rear. Among the group was Colonel Paul Thompson, commander of the 6th Special Engineer Brigade, who had been wounded as he breached the wire obstacles and led his men in an attack to destroy the machinegun position in the house. It was after 0730, but the follow-on waves would have one less dangerous position to deal with.

Hospitalized in England and recovering from his wounds, Colonel Thompson would tell General Bradley, who came to visit him, "So you see, General, there I was with all my responsibilities, going out there and doing the job of a sergeant." "Well Thompson," Bradley responded, "Thank the good Lord there were several Colonels doing the job of sergeants that day." He was undoubtedly thinking about the RCT Commanders on Omaha Beach,

Colonel Thompson, 6th Engineer Special Brigade.

Colonels Canham and Taylor, plus many others who distinguished themselves by leading their men off of the beach on D-Day.

In the third wave of the 116th RCT attack came its 3rd Battalion, which had essentially been held in reserve, prepared to follow and exploit the success of the 1st, and 2nd Battalions. Company L landed first in Easy Green, just to the left of Bingham and the house, which became an easily identifiable landmark. Sergeant Earl Wilkerson of the Headquarters Company 3rd Battalion 116th RCT described the scene. "The craft I was in could only get so close because of all the debris, bodies and stuff. We unloaded in knee-deep water and I hid behind a burning landing craft for protection and for warmth. It was cold, and the heat from the craft felt nice. A lot of other landing craft didn't make it to the shore. I saw some being blown out of the water."

With the tide rising, all of the 3rd Battalion's Companies were offloaded in the rising water inside the obstacle belt. Lieutenant Colonel Lawrence Meeks commanding the 3rd Battalion recalled, "We picked our way through the obstacles. I tried to warn the men that tracer bullets were grazing the beach about a foot above the ground. I gave the order to get across as fast as possible and not to bunch up." The German fire still took its toll as his eight hundred men advanced. Some lay paralyzed against the shingle bank, but a large group, led by Company L, cut an opening in the two strands of barbed wire above and began to make their way up to the top of the cliffs. PFC Norman Grossman of Company L describes what they faced. "The bluff was booby-trapped with anti-personnel mines. We went up the hill single file, for we knew if the man in front of us didn't blow up, we wouldn't either. As we reached the top bullets started whizzing over my head again, and we hit the ground."

In the climb, Sergeant Bernard Lipscomb of Company K saw his best friend walking up the cliff ahead of him step on a mine. "His body was basically blown into pieces and some of his flesh dotted my uniform. I never got over seeing that happen." As they advanced through the minefields, many of the men stepped on bodies or limbs of the unfortunate victims who had gone before them, in order to avoid the same fate.

Within two hours of their landing, elements from all four companies of the 3rd Battalion had reached the high ground where they were joined by members of 2nd Battalion's Company F and G. This was the first wave group that had landed in the wrong place and was still struggling to reach the

Lieutenant Colonel Lawrence E. Meeks, 3/116th. (US Army.)

Pfc Norman Grossman, L/116th RCT, Easy Green. (116th Foundation.)

top. Captain Malcolm R. Weller leading Company L recalled finally reaching the high ground. "I then moved through a field and found part of my battalion which was held up by enemy machine guns and snipers. As things developed, we heard this peculiar thumping about 200 yards to our left. The second look told us it was a rocket position which was firing towards the water. Several of our mortars and machineguns immediately started firing on the rocket guns, but about the same time the navy spotted them and poured the big stuff into the position. That was the end of those rockets."

Sergeant Louis M. Armstrong of Company L wrote of the fight on the high ground, "A number of Germans gave up, but we had to kill most of them to get the ground they held." Often those surrendering would raise their hands and move toward the Americans shouting, "Me Polish, Me Polish." Colonel Canham had issued an order in advance of the landings, directing the men of the 116th RCT to take no prisoners on D-Day. Many of the men, known as "Stonewallers" because their regiment was part of the famous "Stonewall Brigade" during the America Civil War, had no problem following this order, after surviving the carnage of the landings and the struggle up the cliffs and through the minefields. Others, however, accepted the surrender of the defenders and sent them down to the beach to be processed by the military police and become prisoners of war.

For the rest of the morning, the 116th made slow progress and suffered high casualties as they tried to advance across the high ground above Easy Green and Dog Red. They pushed west across the fields, opposed by multiple machine gun positions in the second German line of defense. They were also heavily engaged by fire from artillery and Tobruk mortar positions. The Germans continued a stubborn defense on the high ground of the D-3 draw, where the anti-tank wall prevented any armor advance from the beach. The advancing soldiers of the 2nd and 3rd Battalions would eventually bypass the strongpoint of WN 66 in order to reach the coast road at St. Laurent. It was not until 2000 Hours that engineers finally destroyed the wall and cleared the minefield, allowing tanks to pass through.

Easy Red

The 1,650 yards of beach designated Easy "Red" included the draw known as the Ruquet Valley, or the valley of the Revolution, designated the E-1 Draw. It was the only German strongpoint with WNs in depth. There was WN 65 on the beach to the west, with WN 64 across the valley to the east, defended by elements of 8/916 Grenadiers. Behind WN 65 was WN 67, and above it, just north of the village of St. Laurent, was WN 69. Positioned here was the 84th Werfer Regiment's battery of the very dangerous *Nebelwerfer* rocket launchers, known to the American soldiers as "screaming Meemies." They had been firing effectively on the landing assault force all morning. To the east of the E-1 Draw were over eight hundred yards of open beach. The American Cemetery is now located on the cliffs above this stretch of beach.

WN 65 remains one of the most recognizable positions on Omaha Beach, with an H677 casemate housing a 50mm anti-tank gun, just as it was on D-Day. In addition, there were two Tobruks with mortars and one with a 50 mm anti-tank gun. There was a 75mm gun hidden in a wooden shelter where it could provide enfilading fire on anything entering the Ruquet Valley. Across the draw, the defenses in WN 64 to the east included an H612 casemate, still under construction, with its 76.2 mm Russian field gun positioned nearby. There were also two Tobruk mortar stands and a 20 mm anti-aircraft gun.

Easy Red was the objective of Company E and F of the 16th Infantry Regimental Combat Team. Landing here also, but in error, was Company E, 116th RCT, and a mile from their planned landing objective. In the first wave landing here at H-Hour, 0630, was combat photographer Robert Capa, who would capture the chaos that occurred here.

The beaches of Easy Green today begin with the monument in the Les Moulins Draw and run east to where the hard surface road makes a sharp right hand turn toward the cliffs. The site of the "Bingham House" is under a home nearby the monument as the road turns east just north of the D-Day House Restaurant. The unfinished gun position is hidden in the cliffs above the restaurant. Just below, in the draw was a home occupied by the Ocard family. Local resident Jean Pierre Ocard was only nine when an American soldier knocked on his door the morning of June 6, 1944, "looking for Germans," he recalled. "As they talked to my father, a German soldier passed by the window and the American went outside, took his rifle, had him put his hands over his head, and walked him back down to the beach."

Opposite: Today, in wide view. (G. Bernage.)

Lieutenant John Benz Carroll of the 16th RCT assigned to assist Capa, recalled the scene in his famous photographs, "We would grab out at some of those underwater obstructions and mines built on telephone poles and girders, and hang on. We'd take cover, then make a dash through the surf to the next one, fifty feet away." Capa remembered, "Above the boots and faces, my picture frames were filled with shrapnel, smoke, burnt tanks and sinking barges formed my background."

Easy Red. Robert Capa.

0630. Robert Capa landed with the first assault wave " between the grotesque shapes of steel obstacles.... a narrow strip of sand covered by smoke, our Europe, Easy Red Beach". Facing WN62, a terrible place. He forced his way through the water amid a hail of bullets and managed to take 106 photos, most of which were ruined during development. Only ten were rescued, exceptional pictures snapped at H-hour and here are five of them.

Easy Red.

German machine-guns pinned the Americans to the ground. The tide was rising and this photo was taken roughly half an hour after Robert Capa landed on that sector.

50

They sheltered behind some DD tanks which had been dropped off, one of which had brewed up. (NA/Coll Heimdal).

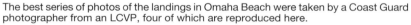

The best series of photos of the landings in Omaha Beach were taken by a Coast Guard photographer from an LCVP, four of which are reproduced here.

1. The LCVP approaches the coast. Each assault company was transported either by 6 LCVP's or 6 LCA's, each of which could carry thirty men. There is a lieutenant of the 1st Inf. Div. in the front on the left who was the platoon commander. The mens' rifles were protected by plastic covers. They were exhausted by the crossing, wracked by sea-sickness and crowded together they suffered from cramp, cold and were drenched through by the waves that broke over them, their feet in a mixture of vomit and sea-water.

2. The approach to the beach. One can see the beach obstacles uncovered by the low tide and the smoke-covered ridge in the background. On the left another LCVP.(PA 26-17), hit by a German shell and emitting a plume of smoke.

3. H-Hour on Easy Red. The landing craft piloted by the Coast Guards landed their soldiers from the 16th RCT between WN62 (left) and WN64 (right) facing the plateau where, after the war, the US cemetery was laid out. We can see in front the landing craft PA 26-18 and PA 26-19 whose men were advancing through the waist deep water.

4. The LCVP from which these photos were taken has just dropped off its infantrymen. One can recognize it from the loop of cable or rope seen in the first photo on the left). On front among the obstacles the men of E/16th and E/116th are all jumbled up having been stopped by the machine-guns of WN62 further to the left. In the centre distance, tank no. 9 of the 741st Tank Battalion can be made out.

(photos NA/coll. Heimdal)

5. Robert Schiska from Mansfield, Ohio, landed at 0730 with the second wave in Easy Red with Company H of the 116th RCT. He can be seen on the right in one of the company's landing craft, on the right of the photo in profile. The vessel is coming in to the beach under WN64 and on the right is the Ruquet valley. (NA/Heimdal).

Also, landing in the first wave was an experienced veteran of the 16th RCT, Private First Class DuWaine J. Raatz, who recalled his first look at Omaha Beach and Easy Red. "I had made two invasions before this, North Africa and Sicily, so I thought I knew a little bit of what it might be like, but in the morning of June 6, 1944, when I saw the beaches of Normandy, France, my spirits dropped. There were stakes, ramps, obstacles, curved rails sticking out of the water. That's when I started to pray and think about what I was going to do."

As artillery and mortar shells began raining down, the soldiers landing raced toward the only possible safety, the base of the high ground ahead. There were no casemates on the beach with heavy direct fire weapons to contend with on Easy Red, like those firing on the landing craft to the west. Still, there were plenty of well-placed machine gun positions providing "grazing fire" across the beach. There was nothing easy about getting across Easy Red. One of the defenders, Corporal Franz Rachmann recalled, "There was thousands of ships, and we could see landing boats of American troops. Then came thousands of men at one time coming on land and running over the beach. This is the first time I shoot on living men, and I go to the machine gun and I shoot, I shoot, I shoot! For each American I see fall, there came ten hundred other ones!"

Private Charles Thomas remembered his coxswain was killed before his boat landed. When the ramp dropped, the young soldier "crawled in over wounded and dead but I couldn't tell who was who and we had orders not to stop for anyone on the edge of the beach, to keep going or we would be hit ourselves." When he finally reached the seawall he recalled, "it was crowded with GIs all being wounded or killed. It was overcrowded with GIs."

Staff Sergeant Donald Wilson of Company F, 2nd Battalion, 16th RCT had reached the seawall on Easy Red and looking back saw LCI 85, carrying personnel of the 1st Medical Battalion in support of the 16th RCT, get hit by German fire. "The explosion sent medics and their gear flying in all direc-

Above is Schiska during a visit to Vierville. (photo. Omaha D-Day Museum, Vierville).

Easy Red

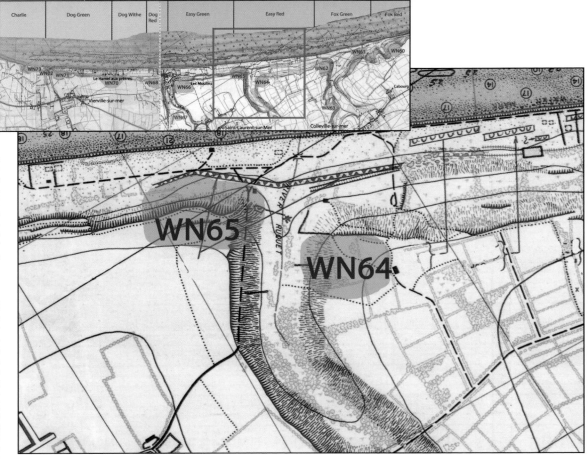

The plan below shows the two positions situated at the entrance to the Ruquet valley. WN 64 was a bit rough and ready, but WN65 had a casemate housing a 50mm gun barring the entrance to the valley and the two weapon pits facing towards the sea. (Map Heimdal).

WN64

Soviet 76.2mm field Gun. On this American photo taken a few months after the landings **(1),** one can see that the sole casemate was only at the foundation stage and the walls consisted only of shuttering and reinforcing material. That casemate was sited to dominate the Ruquet valley and faced the casemate in WN 65 which can be seen at the foot of the escarpment opposite.

Facing north a well preserved stretch of zig-zag trench ran from the artillery position along the crest of the ridge **(2)** on which can be seen concreted niches for ammunition for the 76.2 gun. WN 60 can be made out in the background. (Photo H. Lefèvre).

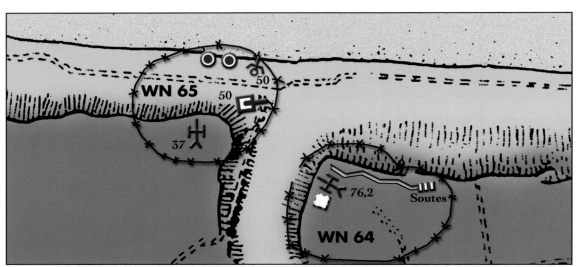

tions. I vividly recall seeing a cloud of white bandages floating down into the smoke on deck." The boat tried to turn back to sea, but in attempting to do so, it became an even bigger target. "As it was broadside, the Jerry gunner resumed firing. The first round was low, but ricocheted off the water, striking the hull," Wilson recounted. "The next two were right at the water line, near midship. The LCI seemed dead in the water."

Captain Joe Dawson, landing in the second wave at 0700 with his Company G, viewed the chaos on Easy Red and feared "E Company and F Company had been virtually decimated." Still he got his men across the beach and headed up the cliffs to follow Lieutenant John Spaulding's platoon of Company E, which had landed off course east of the E-1 Draw. Even further east landing with Company K, Private Roger Brugger recalled, "We ran straight for a shale wall, and as I ran from the boat I saw bullets tearing up the sand on either side of me and I thought, 'This is just like a war movie.' After we got to the shale wall, I looked back at the boat we had just left, when an artillery shell hit it in the engine compartment and blew it up."

Recognizing the situation, Lieutenant Spaulding had taken action. He led his platoon up the steep grade and rushed the machinegun position that had been pouring damaging fire on the troops still pinned on the beach below. The surviving gunner in the position quickly surrendered, becoming one of the first German prisoners of the day. "Kamerad" he shouted with his hands in the air, later he indicated he was Polish. Spaulding recalled, "He said that there were 16 Germans in the area; that they had been alerted that morning and were told they had to hold the beach. They had taken a vote on whether to fight and preferred not to, but the German noncoms made them." Soon a small group appeared to surrender.

Obergrenadier Karl Wegner in WN 62 confirmed the story when he later related that a soldier named Helmuth crawled into his position shouting, "Ich bin Deutscher!" *Obergefreiter*, Corporal Lang in charge of the bunker gave him a drink of water and the distraught man told his story. "He said that in his strongpoint, most of the men were Volksdeutsche, Alsatians and Poles. Things went well until the Amis fired directly at them. Most then refused to fight and demanded that their *Gruppenführer*, group commander, surrender the position. This man, an Obergefreiter, became infuriated and threatened to execute anyone who did not

fight. From behind, one fired a shot and killed him. And since he (Helmuth) was the only 'German' in the Gruppe the man before us was disarmed and beaten up." The group then surrendered to the advancing Americans. When Lang inquired as to the location of his position, Helmuth indicated it was about 100 meters west, near where Lieutenant Spaulding had taken the first prisoner.

In one of the empty German machinegun nests, the Americans found a belt of wooden 7.92 bullets. The incident created the rumor among the GIs, general inductees that the Germans were down to using wooden rounds. In reality, as a result of the lack of raw materials to support the war effort, they did use wooden rounds for practice. The German troops on Omaha Beach had been part of a training exercise and had used the bullets to preserve their limited ammunition supply. The wooden projectiles had only a very short range, but one American soldier recalled being struck in the chest by such a round as he advanced up the hillside of Easy Red.

Spaulding's penetration through the obstacles and minefields, followed by his advance across the high ground, would be one of the first penetrations of the German defenses. Engineers would mark the lane with white tape and soon it would become the main route off Omaha Beach for the 18th RCT and other units that followed. It would be the leadership of young men like Lieutenant Spaulding and courage of individual soldiers that would eventually carry the day for the Americans.

Landing at 0800, Colonel Charles Taylor, commanding the 16th RCT, crossed the beach under heavy machine gun fire. Upon reaching the seawall and finding his soldiers pinned down, he barked to the leaders present, "If we're gonna die, let's do it up there," pointing to the high ground above the beach. For all to hear he shouted, "There are only two kinds of people on this beach: the dead and those about to die. So let's get the hell out of here!" Soon his infantry was up and racing across the open ground beyond the beach which lead to the hilly area beyond.

Captain Fred Gercke, commanding POW Interrogation Team 24, accompanying Colonel Taylor, was with him when the first prisoners were brought down to the beach. Gercke was shocked to learn that the soldiers were from the 352nd Infantry. "This regiment and division were supposed to be about 50 miles south of us, and the only thing our order of battle had told us that we would run into

1. & 2. Two exceptional photos taken on Easy Red by Robert Rieske. The men are pinned down on the shingle bank.

2

1

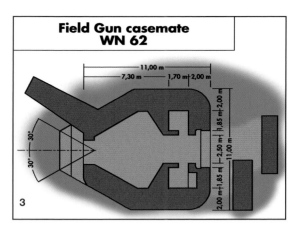

Field Gun casemate WN 62

3

4

1. Two type H669 casemates were constructed in April 1944 to house the pair of Czech 75mm on WN62, following the visit by Rommel. One can see in **(1)** the embrasure of the lower one with its massive side wall to protect it from incoming shells fired from out to sea.

2. Higher and further forward **(2)** the other casemate topped these days by the memorial to the men of the 5th Engineer Brigade.

3. Plan of the type H669 casemate.

4. This is how Rommel found the two Czech 75mm field guns at WN 62 during his visit on 29 January 1944 : standing on concrete platforms, their only protection was a camouflage net slung over two wooden poles. Posing around one of the guns, from left to right, were three soldiers from WN 62, Alois Reckers, Bruno Plota and Hans Selbach. (coll. F Gockel/Heimdal).

at the beach would be the 726th Infantry of the 716th Infantry Division." Captain Gercke immediately informed Colonel Taylor of what he had learned. It would quickly become clear to the American leadership why the fighting on Omaha Beach was so difficult. A tremendous intelligence failure had occurred and the move of the 352nd forward to join the 716th had gone undetected.

Carrier (homing) pigeons sent by the French Resistance had obviously not made it through with the news of the presence of the 352nd. From their experience in World War I, the Germans were keenly aware of the use of pigeons to carry messages and there was a bounty for shooting one down. German officers excelled at skeet shootings, and along with their soldiers using shotguns, the bird's dependability in getting through was questionable. Of the 16,554 pigeons dropped behind German lines, only eleven percent, 1,842, actually made it back to England with a message. From March through May, twenty-seven of the birds had been shot down approaching the Bay of the Seine, from the Resistance base the Germans suspected to be near Criqueville, behind Pointe du Hoc. The interruption to the flow of current intelligence information would prove costly to the V Corps landings on D-Day.

At 0839 Hours, Brigadier General Wyman the Deputy Commander of the 1st Division landed safely and reached the seawall. His first message to General Huebner was a simple, "Beach slow." Observing the chaos before him, he told his aide, "We've got to get these men off the beach. This is murder." In addition to the mass of infantry, much of it still pinned down against the embank-

ment, there were a hundred or more vehicles of every possible description caught in the deadly German fire. There were bulldozers, half-tracks, tanks, anti-aircraft vehicles, even DUKWs trapped on the sand. His next message to the commanding general was more precise, "The beach has too many vehicles. Send combat troops." The response resulted in orders to the 18th RCT and the 115th RCT to prepare to land early, focused on the E-1 Draw.

The engineer GATs came under heavy fire initially and throughout the morning, but continued to work to open lanes in the German obstacle belt. Teams 14, 15, and 16, had been successful in opening multiple gaps in Easy Red, and the lanes attracted far more landing craft than they could handle. The success of the GATs here contributed significantly to the move inland. They were the primary openings for the follow-on soldiers and vehicles landing on Omaha Beach the remainder of D-Day and beyond.

The other great force multiplier, the tanks of the 741st Tank Battalion, commanded by Lieutenant Colonel Robert Skaggs, did not fare as well. Launched from their LCTs at sea at 0530 per the initial operation order, instead of plowing through the rough water at five knots, fourteen of the Company B tanks sank straight to the bottom of the Bay of the Seine. Corporal Wardell Hopper was in the first tank to launch and followed it to the bottom. "I will never forget my cigarettes coming out of my pocket and going past my face; that is when

I started breathing water, and thought I was gone." Inflating his Mae West saved his life and brought him to the surface near where he had launched. "Then the LCT threw me a line. I had to wrap it around my arms, because my hands were too cold. They pulled me aboard and I pass out."

Only two of the Shermans were able to float in, and three others arrived on an LCT that observed the disaster and delivered the precious cargo directly to the beach. Many tankers were lost, but one sailor watching the site recalled, "The guys started popping up like corks." On his way to the beach, Captain Fred Hall, S-3 of the 2nd Battalion 16th RCT, saw some crews floating in their yellow life rafts and quickly realized "that meant that we would not have tank support on the beach." Armor support would be limited until the work of the GATs would allow tanks to be deposited directly onto the sand.

Still, the tanks that made it in were effective in destroying some of the big guns protecting the E-3 Draw. Sergeant George Geddes in one of the tanks that floated in, engaged and destroyed the two encased 75mm guns in WN 62. Nearby, Staff Sergeant Turner Sheppard in the second tank, took out the 88mm gun positioned in the casemate of WN 61. Their kills would be disputed by members of First Lieutenant Edward Sledge's Platoon of three tanks offloaded from their LCT onto Easy Red. They took credit for the destruction of the encased guns at 0715. In addition, soldiers of Company F, 16 RCT credited Staff Sergeant Frank Strojny with putting eight bazooka rounds into one of the positions. In any event, three very dangerous German guns were destroyed, but artillery and mortar rounds continued to fall and several 50mm antitank positions remained firing and keeping the infantry pinned down.

The line of soldiers piling up on the beach was observed by the Navy Lieutenant Commander James Semmes of the USS Frankford who took action. Running his ship dangerously close to shore, dragging bottom, on occasion only 900 yards offshore, he ordered his gunnery officer Lieutenant Owen Keeler to locate and engage the German defenders of E-1. Visibility was poor, but Keeler remembered, "Then one of our light tanks that was sitting at the water's edge with a broken track fired at something on the hill. We immediately followed up with a five-inch salvo. The tank gunner flipped open his hatch, waved, dropped back in the tank and fired at another target. For the next few minutes, he was our fire-control party. Our rangefinder optics could examine the spots where his shells hit."

Sergeant James Knight of the 299th Engineer Combat Battalion on the beach, was exuberant over the work of the USS Frankford, "She started to turn right, and before she completed the turn to be parallel to the beach, all her guns opened fire." The soldiers pinned beneath the cliffs could see the rounds passing just above their heads and striking the concrete emplacements above. As he lay wounded on the beach, Captain Charles Murphy of the 1st Engineer Combat Battalion observed, "We saw them go right in there. Boy, that was the end. I loved the Navy from then on."

Captain Carroll recalled the Navy's role in the destruction of numerous German positions that had been so effective against the American soldiers landing in Easy Red. "The emplacements

The small valley which is actually the stepped footpath leading up to the cemetery, was used by the men who had landed on Easy Red to reach the plateau. (aerial photo by Romeo India).

were being completely destroyed, and chunks of cement as big as a foot square were falling all around us and on us. The shells were coming in no higher than 100ft over our heads. They hit and blew that cliff right out." Colonel S. B. Mason, Chief of Staff of the 1st Division, would later write, "Without that gunfire we positively could not have crossed the beaches." The dangerous 88mm cannon in WN 61 was recorded destroyed at 0720.

Soon Colonel Mason was able to report, "They are falling back little by little." On the German side, a very concerned *Oberst* Goth reported to *Generalleutnant* Kraiss, "Naval guns are smashing up our strong-points. We are running short of ammunition. We urgently need supplies, Herr General." Before the message was acknowledged, the line went dead. The continuous firing was also taking its toll on the German defenders' capability to communicate. Still, there was little Kraiss could do to assist. Breakthroughs were occurring across the broad Allied landing front, and there were insufficient reserves to respond.

Effective fire came from other unplanned sources. Battery A, 467th Anti-Aircraft Battalion was tasked to land in E-1, proceed up the draw, and set up their guns on the cliffs above. They landed safely, but amid the chaos in Easy Red. Sergeant Hyman Haas spotted a pillbox dug into the hillside, wreaking havoc on the beach. His M-15 half-track was armed with a 37mm cannon with twin 50mm machine guns. The guns were angled up to fire at aircraft, so the cab of the vehicle prevented it from firing straight ahead. Using good old American ingenuity, Haas turned his vehicle and proceeded down the beach until he could find a low place for the wheels which would provide the angle necessary to fire on the position. "My first three shots were low. I took the antiaircraft range and clicked that off and raised my sights three clicks. The next ten shots went directly into the porthole of the pillbox." This is the type H667 casemate that remains in place today.

Above: at Tidworth on 9 April 1944 the men of the 121st Engineer Bn. try out a flame-trower. (DAVA/Heimdal)

Opposite: panoramic view taken from the American cemetery, the route used to climb on the plateau, left, and the WN62, right. (G. Bernage)

The casemate H667 in June 1944… (NA)

… and today. (G. Bernage)

Private First Class Leroy Hermann of Company A landed in the 16th RCT's third wave at 0750. It was made up of the entire 1st Battalion. Like many others, the young soldier struggled through the rising tide and finally found safety in an artillery hole when he reached the sand. "I crawled into a shell hole to dry out a bit because the landing craft had let us off in deep water and we were soaked."

Company B landed behind Company A. 16th RCT veteran Sergeant John Ellery described the scene as the "greatest concentration of mortar, machine-

The casemate defending the WN65 and the entrance of Ruquet Valley. (E. Groult/Heimdal)

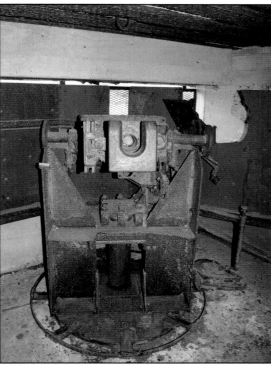

The 50 mm gun today, outside and inside. (E. Groult/G. Bernage.)

gun, and artillery fire I had ever seen." Staff Sergeant Harley Reynolds moved across the beach and up the cliffs behind WN 64. Looking back at the beach beyond the E-1 Draw he saw "It filled with vehicles and troops. The troops were streaming inland."

Company C landing further east still faced active German positions. "The enemy fire was really heavy," recalled Private Buddy Mazzara of Company C, "and many of our buddies were killed or wounded as we crossed the open beach to get behind the little bluff." He used the flamethrower he was carrying on the aperture of a German machinegun position and recalled, "Soon some soldiers came out of the pillbox with their hands up saying, 'No shoot. No shoot. Me Pole.'"

To his left, east, Lieutenant Spaulding was now leading his men in an advance toward Colleville. They joined Captain Dawson and Company G from the first wave, now well inland and moving south. Company E and G would lead the attack toward the Church steeple they could see in the middle of the village of Colleville.

At 1040, the Beach master on Easy Red radioed to the Navy command group to "send in H+195 wave at once." This message would be followed at 1115 Hours by, "Inf advancing send reinforcements." E-1 was now essentially open and General Wyman's request being filled. The 2nd Battalion of the 18th RCT was soon arriving to the right of the E-1 Draw in 18 LCVPs. Like the LCAs, the LCVP carried about a platoon-sized organization, thirty soldiers. Later waves of RCTs would arrive in LCIs, which were capable of transporting two hundred fighters, more than one company per boat.

They would be followed by the 1st and 2nd Battalions of the 115th RCT coming in on the right side of the draw, exactly where the first wave of the 16th RCT had landed at H-Hour. The 3rd Battalion followed them at 1200. As his boat approached the beach, Private Gene Cogan of Company B, 115th knew why his company commander had told them to write a letter home the night before. "It might be your last," the Captain said; "now I knew why." The 115th came onto Easy Red in 12 LCIs, many of which remained to begin the evacuation of the wounded being treated on the beach.

At 1223, the 1st Battalion of the 18th RCT landed just to the right of the 115th. They were also in LCIs and will be followed by the 3rd Battalion at 1330. Landing this way would require the 18th RCT units to turn east to support the attack into Colleville, while the 115th moved west toward St. Laurent. The dangerous crossing of lines occasionally resulted in "friendly fire" incidents. Another tragedy resulted when misdirected naval gunfire struck the Americans as they climbed the cliffs to get off of Omaha Beach.

As the 18th RCT arrived in Easy Red, Staff Sergeant Walter Ehlers of Company E recalled, "We got on the beach and they have all these people laying down on the beach that were killed. It was chaos." He had no way of knowing that one of the bodies in the sand not far away was that of his older brother Roland, who had landed earlier with Company K in LCI 487. An experienced combat veteran from his two other landings with the 1st Division, Sergeant Ehlers would lead his squad up the cliff and, jumping into the German trench line, attack and destroy a machinegun position that had been taking a deadly toll on the Americans. This action on D-Day earned him a Bronze Star Medal, and moving inland, only three days later, he would earn America's top award, the Congressional Medal of Honor. It wasn't until July that he would learn of his brother's death. "Roland and I were good buddies, he was always kind of looking out for me. He was MY hero."

At 1130, the E-1 Draw was declared open, but not cleared. Soon engineers would build a road in the hill behind WN 65, and by 1700 they had opened the draw wide enough to allow tanks to begin rolling off of the beach.

Having war correspondents embedded with Army units was a new concept, which allowed Gordon Gaskill to land on Easy Red. He wrote, "The beach was strewn with abandoned equipment. Almost instantly men had thrown away their packs, which averaged a little less than 100 pounds each. It was sheer idiocy to think of running such a gauntlet with such an enormous burden." His most vivid memory though was the line of corpses on the beach. "I walked along slowly, counting the bodies. Within 400 paces I counted 221 of them." Easy Red would be nicknamed, "Easy Black."

Easy Red will always live through the photographs of Robert Capa. The western edge of this sector begins at the monument and runs east 850 yards along Rue Bernard Anquetil. As the road makes a sharp turn to the right, this is the beginning of Easy Red, which will take you to WN 65, the E-1 Draw, and the casemate which still contains the 50mm antitank gun. Brush and sand dunes prevent you from seeing the beach from here, but on D-Day, this gun was perfectly positioned to fire on anything landing to the east.

The 75mm cannon and machinegun positions of WN 64 were located on the eastern side of the draw, now covered by brush. Further east on the high ground is the American Cemetery. You can park and walk to the stretch of beach to the east below the Cemetery, which was the most lightly defended site on D-Day.

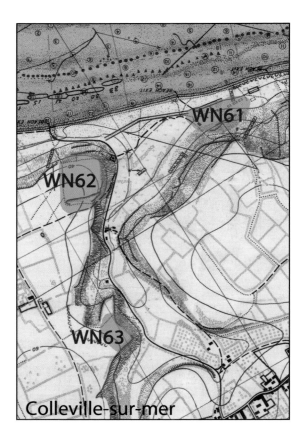

Colleville-sur-mer

Fox Green

The beach designated as Fox "Green" was 1130 yards wide and included the important E-3 Draw leading to the town of Colleville. This was the site of the concrete works of the Todt Company which had constructed the casemates and pillboxes on Omaha Beach. The Draw was defended by the very strong WN 61 and WN 62 with their dangerous direct and indirect fire capability, and a company headquarters and communications center positioned in WN 63 in Colleville. WN 62 west of the draw housed the Observation Post critical to the German artillery and included two type H669 casemates with Czech 75mm guns. There were two Tobruk mortar positions and one with a machinegun. There were also two 50mm Tobruk antitank cannons. It also included two water-cooled Polish machineguns and one MG34 and one MG42 in the open. There were machinegun positions on the high ground designated WN 62A, located in the eastern portion of the American Cemetery and WN 62B on the western side. WN 62 was manned by 27 members of the 3/726 Grenadiers.

Also in the position were thirteen soldiers from the 1st Battery, 1st Battalion of the 352nd Artillery Regiment, which included radio operators, and forward observers. They were housed in a concrete OP along with their Battery Commander, *Oberleutnant* (First Lieutenant) Bernard Frerking. A short distance away was a bunker housing Corporal Hein Severloh and his MG42. One of the unique features of WN 62 was the gravel mill located on the beach, with a conveyor belt to carry the crushed stone to a narrow gauge rail system, which supplied construction sites at WN 61 still being built.

On the eastern portion of the Draw in WN 61 was the second 88mm Pak 43 gun in an H677 casemate that interlocked with the one located in

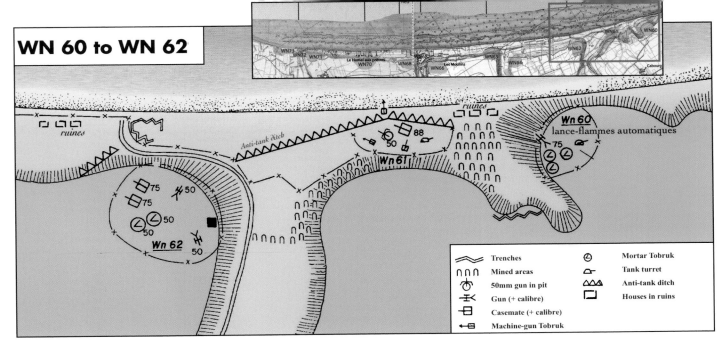

WN 60 to WN 62

Wn 60 lance-flammes automatiques
Wn 61
Wn 62

Anti-tank ditch
ruines
ruines

Symbol	Meaning	Symbol	Meaning
〜〜〜	Trenches	⊘	Mortar Tobruk
∩∩∩	Mined areas	⌐	Tank turret
⊕	50mm gun in pit	△△△	Anti-tank ditch
⊁	Gun (+ calibre)	⊏⊐	Houses in ruins
⊟	Casemate (+ calibre)		
⊡	Machine-gun Tobruk		

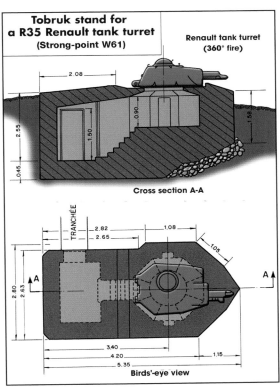

Tobruk stand for a R35 Renault tank turret
(Strong-point W61)

Renault tank turret (360° fire)

Cross section A-A

TRANCHEE

Birds'-eye view

WN71. The position also housed a Tobruk Renault 35 tank turret, an encased 50mm anti-tank gun, and two Tobruks with machineguns and two flamethrowers. A tank ditch stretched across the E-3 opening, supported by a minefield further up the draw.

In WN 62, eighteen-year-old German defender *Grenadier* (Private) Franz Gockel recalled, "It was about 6am when lots of them started up the beach towards me. They came at low tide when we had expected them to come at high tide. They had a long way to go up the sand and hardly any cover. It was a beautiful sandy beach, and they had to run all the way up it." *Obergrenadier* (Pfc) Karl

The 5cm Pak gun (26 on the map) with which Siegfried Kuska could sweep the beach between WN 62 and 61. As this photo, taken after the landings, shows, it was emplaced in a fold of the ground and could not be located by the Americans – it remained intact. (NA Archives).

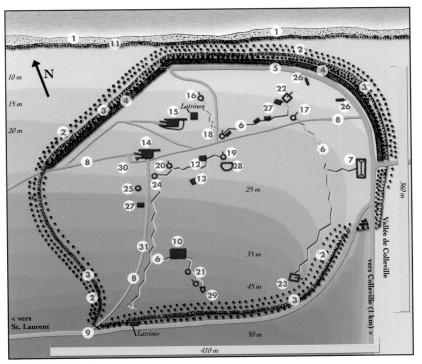

vers St. Laurent
Latrines
vers Colleville (1 km) >
Vallée de Colleville

WN62 - 1. Shingle. **2.** Mines. **3.** Barbed wires. **4.** Antitank ditch, full of water. **5.** Northern way. **6.** Trenches. **7.** Ward-Post and kitchen. **8.** East/west and south way. **9.** South entrance. **10.** Underground troop shelter. **11.** Antitank-wall. **12.** Observation bunker for Artillery Regiment 352 (B. Frerking). **13.** Bunker for signals, connection with AR352. **14.** Upper casemate for 75 mm gun. **15.** Under casemate for 75 mm gun. **16, 17, 18, 19** and **20.** Tobruk for machine-gun. **21.** Double tobruk for mortar and machine-gun (see next page). **22** and **23.** Field position for 50 mm gun. **24** and **25.** Tobruk for 50 mm mortar (see next page). **26.** 50 mm antitank gun. **27.** Bunker for munitions. **28.** Old position for 75mm gun. **29.** Concrete mounting for a signal lamp. **30.** 5th Special Engineers Brigade Monument. (Map Heimdal).

Lt. Frerking (above) commanded the 1st Battery of the 352nd Artillery Regiment. To follow operations he went to WN62 on 6 June accompanied by his batman, Severloh (below), although they did not know the infantry at that position. There they met up with the artillery observation team consisting of Lt. Grass as well as Sergeant Fak and the two radio operators.

Wagner froze when the first wave of the 16 RCT landed and he heard the order "*Feuer*, Wagner, *Feuer*!" Then he recalled, "The MG roared, sending hot lead into the men running along the beach. I saw some go down, I knew I had hit them. Others dived for whatever cover was out there. The bullets ripped up and down the sand.

Nearby, in his observation bunker Lieutenant Frerking commanded, "*Dora, Feuer*!" The order identified the position of the landing force for the four guns of his 105 batteries located almost three miles inland at Houtteville. The German high command was convinced the Allied landings would occur during high tide, but still the artillery was zeroed in and ready for every possible landing scenario. Preplanned "Dora," targeted the water line at low tide, exactly where the American boats were touching the sand. On the order, the other defenders of WN 62, with a perfect view of the landings, also began their deadly direct fire on the assault force.

Twenty-one year old Corporal Severloh, who had served on the Russian front, was manning his position half way up the hill in WN 62 when the order came. "We had strict orders to wait until the GIs were only about 400 meters from the edge of the beach," he recalled, "and were wading in water up to their knees." The later waves would be handled a bit differently. "As the boats approached, I concentrated on the ramps. As soon as they came down for the GIs to jump out, I began to fire. With the tide rising, the landing craft came even closer to the edge of the beach. The GIs tried to find cover behind the beach obstacles which towered above the waves, or corpses of their fallen comrades which were washing up and down."

Landing in front of WN 62 came the boats of Company E and F of the 16th RCT as well as Company E of the 116th RCT, which were well east of their landing objective in Dog Red. It became a target-rich environment for the well-positioned Severloh. "After the landing craft offloaded their living cargo on to the beach, they withdrew. Until the next wave arrived, I fired at everything which moved in the water and on the beach. I sometimes used my carbine, since I could fire aimed shots at individual soldiers and at the same time give my machine gun a chance to cool down."

Captain Lawrence Madill and four boats of his Company E, 116th RCT landed by mistake in Fox Green west of the E-3 draw. Private Harry Parley

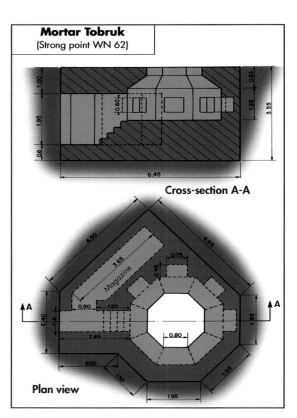

Mortar Tobruk
(Strong point WN 62)

Cross-section A-A

Plan view

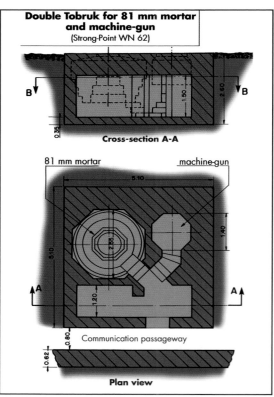

Double Tobruk for 81 mm mortar and machine-gun
(Strong-Point WN 62)

Cross-section A-A

81 mm mortar   machine-gun

Communication passageway

Plan view

On this photo taken facing north one can see on the right the double Tobruk for mortar and machine-gun. In the foreground is the exit from the underground troop shelter and on the left is the concreted communication passageway. In the background is the concrete mounting for a signal lamp. Right in the background, roughly a kilometre distant the church tower of Colleville is visible.

Private Harry Parley, age 24, E Company, 116th RCT. (Coll. H. Parley)

remembered the struggle to get across the beach. "The Germans were directing their fire down onto the beach so that the line of advancing attackers would run into it and, since I was behind, I was ignored." Flopping onto the shingle embankment, he went on. "Men were trying to dig or scrape trenches or foxholes for protection from the mortars." Severely wounded while trying to rally his men to get up and run to the base of the cliffs, Madill's last words were "Senior noncom, take the men off the beach!"

Private First Class Bernard Nider recalled the idea his buddy Fred Bitsig had, that helped them get across the beach. "Fred said the next time a shell hits, we will head for the hole while the sand is up in the air. So we did this a couple of times and then got the idea of throwing out one of the satchel charges and blowing the sand up in the air and by God it worked. We made it to the sea wall and were about the first ones to make it. I still wonder how Fred and I missed all that lead that was in the air. It was a real slaughter."

It wasn't just the 116th RCT boats that got caught in the strong easterly current. Company I of the 16th RCT was scheduled to land in Fox Green to open the E-3 Draw. Known to the locals as the Les Moulins Draw, it led to the town of Colleville which is the name it was best known by. The easterly Channel current swept the entire Company I down the Norman coast toward the British sector "Gold" at Port en Bessin. Two of the boats would be lost when they struck obstacles hidden in the rising tide. The remaining four boats would arrive late in Fox Green to disembark their cargo of water-soaked, exhausted soldiers. The rough water also took its toll on the tanks of Company C, 741st Armor Battalion that were to float onto Dog Green beach in the first wave just ahead of the infantry. Launched 5,000 yards from the beach, almost every tank immediately plunged straight to the bottom of the Bay of the Seine.

Learning from the disaster, additional tanks were landed directly onto the beach from their LCMs. Private First Class Albert Littke of the 299th Engineer Combat Battalion aboard one of these craft recalled the ride to the beach. "Going in, the battleships and smaller boats were laying down a huge barrage. Looking out to my right, I noticed an LCT with large tubes-rocket launchers- on it. I watched them firing toward the beach. They fired clusters of rockets, which you could see for a split second, coming out of the tubes about every two seconds." He was also impressed by the guns of the battleship USS Texas. Each blast seemed to shake his small landing boat.

Private Albert Mominee of Company I recalled his boat finally landing. "By the time we went in, we were two hours late and the tide had started to come in and cover the obstacles in our path. This made it very hard to single them out and avoid them. About four hundred yards from shore, the craft gave a sudden lurch as it hit an obstacle, and in an instant an explosion erupted, followed by a blinding flash of fire. The LCI was enveloped in flames." The boat sank almost immediately, leaving its occupants floating in the surf. "Before I knew it, I was in the water," Mominee went on, "and had pulled the release straps on my combat jacket and let it slip into the water. Next I inflated the life preserver around my waist and moved away from the craft towards the shore."

LCIs could carry almost 200 men. Some of them suffered a tragic end, victims of German artillery and mines. This was the case with LCI 91 which came in with the second wave and LCI(L) which beached at 1115. The above painting shows LCI 93 in front of WN62 and one can see the house used as a kitchen. (US Navy). NA/Heimdal)

Members of Company I finally reached the shingle bank and ledge on the edge of the sand to get out of the line of fire. Observing their effort to hide, Private Gockel in WN 62 recalled, "The safety offered the attackers was only temporary, for our mortars lay deadly fire upon preset coordinates along the wall. Mortar rounds with impact fuzes exploded on target. The shell splinters, wall fragments, and stones inflicted casualties upon the troops." The preplanned German fires across Omaha Beach had deadly effects throughout the morning.

In the meantime the companies, which had landed on time in the first and second waves, were practically destroyed by the fire from WN 62. Medic Ray Lambert of the 2nd Battalion recalled that "Soldiers were going down left and right, and I remember feeling overwhelmed. I couldn't get to them all to help them, and that was a horrible feeling. Effectively Fox Company ceased to exist as a military unit." Dragging wounded to the limited safety of the concrete works, he is wounded three times but remembered vividly, "Stationary rocks being turned into lethal projectiles by exploding mortar shells." Nearby his brother Ryan would also become a casualty of the indirect fire and the two would spend months side by side in an English Hospital recovering from their wounds.

Private Joseph Argenzio of Company M recalled a scene of horror that occurred with many soldiers and landing boats. "We hit something and they dropped the ramp. The guys in front got killed right away because the Germans had it zeroed in with cross-fire with machineguns and everything. Somebody said, 'Go over the side' so I went over the side and right to the bottom. Goodbye helmet, goodbye carbine, goodbye ammunition cans. I started to crouch down in the water that came up towards the beach and there were dead bodies

Aerial view of the position, half way up the slope showing part of WN 62 with the two casemates **(14)** to the left and **(15)** to the right. On the extreme left the observation post **(12)** and the empty emplacement **(28)** can be made out. (J Soucy/ Romeo India).

Franz Gockel.

Lt. Hans Heinze.

all around so I laid down and grabbed two of them which were right in front of me. They were dead. They were mutilated but they saved my life."

WN 62 fought tenaciously throughout the morning and into the afternoon. Private Gockel, who manned one of the Polish machine guns, remembered that he, "stayed there until about midday on my own until a commander called Siegfried came and asked me to go up to the bunker and get him something to eat." Exposing himself to the American fire, he raced up the hill where he enjoyed lunch with two other defenders. "I wanted to go back to Siegfried, but the Americans were already there. They had taken the position." Soon he would be wounded in the hand and evacuated to the rear for treatment.

When Company H, 16 RCT arrived, the German firing had begun to diminish. Still, there were casualties. One tragic loss could have been prevented. Private First Class Cecil Painter recalled a member of his mortar squad "dropped the base plate of the 81mm mortar on a German mine and blew himself up." Crossing the beach was still not completely safe when the 1st Division's heavy weapons and equipment began arriving.

Meanwhile, a German counter attack was being organized to drive the Americans back to the sea. Ordered at 1200, it took until 1300 to get the move underway, led by First Lieutenant Heller, commanding Company 6/916. He was wounded leading the attack, and remnants of his unit were combined with survivors in Company 5/916 and 8/916 to attempt another counterattack under the command of First Lieutenant Hans Heinze, Colonel Goth's chief logistician and aide. He divides his command into three groups, two assaulting and one providing covering fire.

At 1400, the 916th Regiment sends the following report to the 352nd Division. "5/GR 916 has stopped the enemy breakthrough between

WN62a, b and 64 with a counter attack and is leading the attack of II Batt." Successful initially, Lieutenant Heinze was able to recapture much of the high ground, which today is the site of the American Cemetery. Before long though, his force is pounded by naval gunfire. He recalled "Soon the Americans bombarded us with all they had. After a long time I knew we couldn't hold out any longer. I ordered the men to try to get out through the shelling by themselves, not in groups. This was the only possible way through that terrible fire." Leading another counter attack later in the evening, Heinze became cut off from the rest of the 916th Regiment. He would remain behind American lines for the next two days, observing their movements before escaping to report his observations to Colonel Goth and receive a new assignment.

Corporal Severloh stayed in his position until after 1500 when an American force began clearing out the bunkers in WN 62. Lieutenant Frerking finally orders a retreat and is killed trying to make his escape. His artillery battery had gotten down to their "emergency reserve" which allowed them to fire only three rounds and only when a *Stützpunkt* was in danger of being overrun. When this ammunition reserve was exhausted, the guns would be destroyed and the gunners would escape on the horses used to pull the battery. Moving the guns was out of the question and all efforts to resupply the guns had been thwarted by the *Jagdbombers*, German soldiers called *"Jabos,"* Allied fighter-bombers were now actively patrolling the area behind the beach. Their efforts during the afternoon of D-Day were invaluable in preventing not only German resupply efforts, but stopping any effective reinforcement of the German main-line of defense.

LCI 83 was hit for the first time at 0830, off Fox Green and it was unable to beach and transfer 72 men of the 20th Engineer Battalion. It finally got in at 1115 hrs. as can be seen here. It received a shell on the port side which killed 16 men and was further damaged by a mine while landing its troops, but was re-floated that same evening.

Severloh avoided the same fate as his commander, but was wounded as he escaped exhausted to the headquarters of 915th Grenadier Regiment in WN 63 commanded by Major/Doctor Lohmann. Co-located here was the headquarters of the 3/726 Grenadiers, commanded by Lieutenant Bauch. Severloh received medical aid in the command bunker that also served as a *Funkstation*, or communications center, for the two units. He informed the officers present that WN 62 had fallen, and then lay down to rest with other wounded. As night set in, the survivors assembled in WN 63 realize

they must use the darkness to escape further inland. Taking the few American prisoners they have, Major Lohmann led the group through Colleville, but they were quickly spotted by soldiers of the 1st Division and taken prisoners of war themselves.

At 1630, resistance in the E-3 Draw had ended and engineers began filling in the tank ditches and opening a road inland. It was 0100, the morning of 7 June before the draw was finally declared open to traffic.

Fox Green is the best-preserved German defensive site on Omaha Beach. The parking to the left of the end of the Route de la Mer from Colleville will allow you to reach the beach easily to see the remains of the Todt concrete works. Up the hill are the positions of WN 62, where you can still find the two large 75mm casemates as well as the bunker of Lieutenant Frerking and Corporal Severloh's machinegun position.

Driving back to the east, turn down toward the La Belambra Club. Park here and walk down the road to the beach to find WN 61. The dangerous German 88 mm gun position remains intact, but the embrasure is covered with wood. The gun was removed after the war and melted down along with almost all of the other large weapons the Germans had defending Omaha Beach. Above the casemate is the position of the 50mm antitank gun and machinegun trenches. The beach from here east reflects the shingle embankment similar to the one present today across most of Omaha Beach on D-Day. It turns into the steep cliffs, which protected many American soldiers as they landed and later became an important medical treatment area.

As you drive west from this site, note the ditch on your right, which was a deep tank ditch on D-Day to prevent armor from getting off of the beach. Like all of the German strong points, WN 62 before you was surrounded by wire obstacles and contained a zigzag ditch allowing defenders to move from one position to another inside the position. Proceed up the hill to the Normandy American Cemetery and Memorial, an absolute "must visit!" The Visitor's Center captures the stories of many American heroes who fought in Normandy, and a walk through the Cemetery will provide an forgettable experience.

Engineers

Bangalore torpedo connecting sleeve and cap found in dunes at Vierville-sur-mer

Card cover for a 1-pound block of TNT, used among other things to destroy beach obstacles.

US booby trap wire also used for triggering German mines at a safe distance.

Rubberized boots issued to Engineers for amphibious operations.

Crimping pliers for detonators.

Box for detonators.

Wrapping for electric detonators.

Bag issued to Engineers for carrying detonators and other demolition items.

British-made barbed wire cutters and 'US' carrier.

(Fonds Fantastic Attic/Bayeux.)

67

Infantry

29th Infantry Division helmet.

1st Infantry Division patch.

29th Infantry Division patch.

Rubberized waterproof backpack for carrying radio equipment during amphibious operations.

29th Infantry Division helmet liner.

Rubberized assault gas mask bag for amphibious operations.

Inflatable life belt worn by each soldier during landing operations. This example was found in a house at Vierville-sur-mer during the 1990's.

(Fonds Fantastic Attic/Bayeux.)

New Testament with metal 'shield' cover supposed to stop a bullet. Normally carried in the left breast shirt pocket to protect the heart.

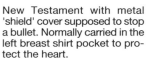

Waxed cardboard K-Ration breakfast unit.

Waxed cardboard K- Ration supper unit.

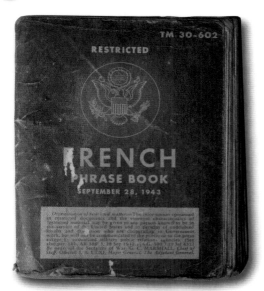

Pack of "Lucky Strike" cigarettes.

French phrase book with phonetic pronunciation to be able to communicate with the French.

Can of beer.

Chewing-gun profusely distributed by the GI's to the Norman population. This example was kept as a souvenir by an inhabitant of Trévières.

Omaha Beach
Le 04 Mars 2010

1. 29th Infantry Division helmet liner found in a house at Vierville-sur-mer.

2. 29th Infantry Division helmet found in close proximity to the beach at Vierville-sur-mer.

3. First aid packet tin found in the dunes at Saint-Laurent-sur-mer.

4. Ration can lid found intact in the dunes at Saint-Laurent-sur-mer in 2010. It was protected for 66 years

5. Eye piece of a sight from a DD tank. It was found on the beach at Saint-Laurent-sur-mer during a winter storm.

6. "Walkie-Talkie" found in a shipwreck. It was brought up in the nets of a fishing boat.

(Fonds Fantastic Attic/Bayeux.)

Fox Red

The most easterly position on Omaha Beach was designated Fox "Red." It stretched over 3,000 yards east to Port en Bessin. The German strong point here protected the beach exit the Allies identified as F-1. The exit was also covered partially by the defenses of WN 61, but primarily by WN 60 located here with the usual beach obstacles and several zig-zag trenches above the short cliff where the beach ended. There were three Tobruks with mortars, one additional mortar in the open, one 75mm gun covering the beach to the west, and one 20mm antiaircraft gun in a pit in the center of the position. There were also several positions prepared for 75mm guns, but fortunately for the Americans landing here, only one had arrived by June 6, 1944. WN 60 consisted of forty defenders from the 3/726 Grenadiers, commanded by

First Sergeant Hans Eberhard. In a command bunker on the high ground above this position and further east, Major Werner Pluskat, commanding the 352nd Artillery, spotted the Allied fleet as depicted by Cornelius Ryan in *"The Longest Day."*

There were no planned first wave landings into Fox Red, but the strong easterly Channel current swept Company L of the 16th RCT from their planned site in Fox green, east into Fox Red, right below WN 60. Landing thirty minutes late, Private Steve Kellman recalled, "As we got in closer, we could hear the machine-gun bullets hitting the

WN60 - This zig-zag trench is still easily visible, looking east. (David Ashe).

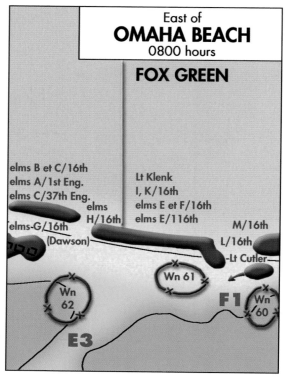

From WN60 there is an exceptional view on the strand below and of the entire stretch of Omaha Beach sector. (David Ashe).

sides of the vessel and the ramp in front." As the ramps dropped, Captain John R. Armellino, commanding the company led his men toward the base of the cliffs, but was seriously wounded by mortar fire as he organized the attack to destroy WN 60. Command passed to the company Executive Officer, Lieutenant Robert Cutler, Jr. He organized the assault into sections; one would head west into the F-1 Draw and defilade cover from observation by the German defenders, while a second would be set up to provide supporting fire.

After 125 survivors of Company L got organized, Lieutenant Kenneth Klink led the first section in their advance to the high ground behind WN 60. Lieutenant Cutler called for naval gunfire and the destroyer USS Doyle immediately responded effectively pinning down the German defenders. His critical communications with the Navy was a result of the brave action of Technician 5th Class John J. Pinder, Jr. This soldier's determination and ultimate sacrifice earned him the first Congressional Medal awarded for the events of D-Day. After crossing the beach safely, he returned several times to locate communication equipment dropped during the landing. The citation reads, "Remaining exposed to heavy enemy fire, growing steadily weaker, he aided in establishing the vital radio communication on the beach. While so engaged this dauntless soldier was hit for the third time and killed."

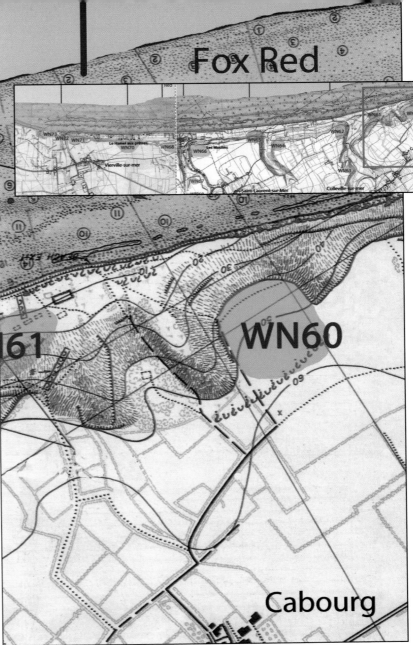

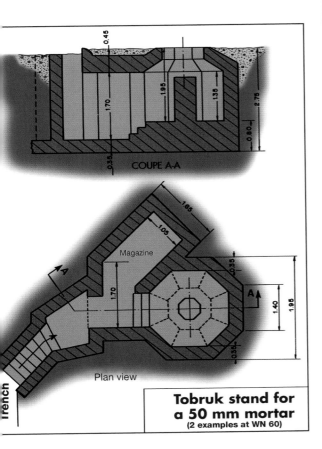

COUPE A-A

Magazine

Plan view

Tobruk stand for a 50 mm mortar
(2 examples at WN 60)

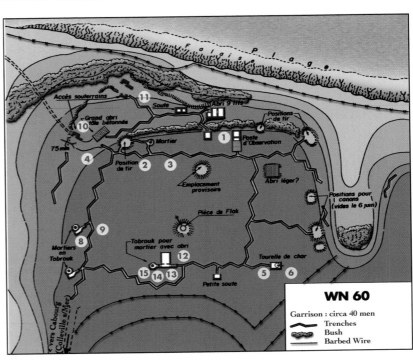

WN 60

Garrison : circa 40 men

Trenches
Bush
Barbed Wire

1. Observation Post. **2.** Trenches (see picture on the opposite page). **4.** Step to 75mm field gun. **5.** Trench to tobruk. **6.** Tobruk with tank turret. **8.** Two Tobruks for mortar (map above). **9.** Trench. **10.** Light Shelter. **12.** Shelter and mortar pit. **13, 14, 15.** Trenches… (Heimdal map.)

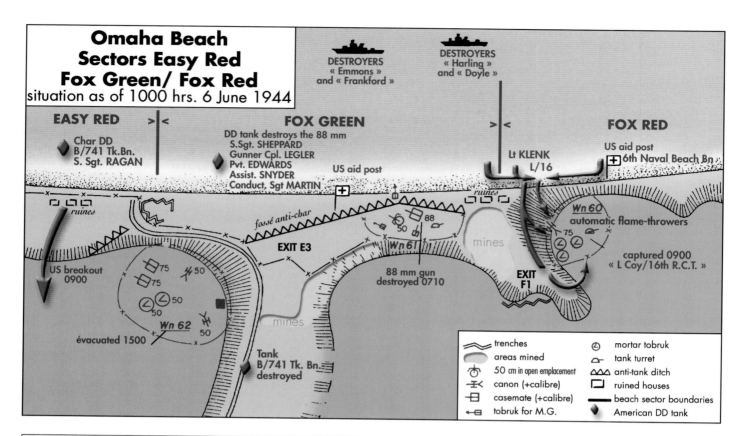

Omaha Beach Sectors Easy Red Fox Green/ Fox Red
situation as of 1000 hrs. 6 June 1944

DESTROYERS « Emmons » and « Frankford »

DESTROYERS « Harling » and « Doyle »

EASY RED

Char DD
B/741 Tk.Bn.
S. Sgt. RAGAN

US breakout
0900

75
75
50
50
Wn 62
50

évacuated 1500

Tank
B/741 Tk. Bn.
destroyed

FOX GREEN

DD tank destroys the 88 mm
S.Sgt. SHEPPARD
Gunner Cpl. LEGLER
Pvt. EDWARDS
Assist. SNYDER
Conduct, Sgt MARTIN

US aid post

fossé anti-char

EXIT E3

88
50

Wn 61

88 mm gun
destroyed 0710

mines

FOX RED

Lt KLENK
L/16

US aid post
6th Naval Beach Bn

mines

Wn 60
automatic flame-throwers

75

EXIT
F1

captured 0900
« L Coy/16th R.C.T. »

ruines

	trenches		mortar tobruk
	areas mined		tank turret
	50 cm in open emplacement		anti-tank ditch
	canon (+calibre)		ruined houses
	casemate (+calibre)		beach sector boundaries
	tobruk for M.G.		American DD tank

These men, armed with a heavy machine-gun are setting off westwards, probably to attack WN60. (DAVA, Coll. Heimdal.)

Sergeant James Knight in SETF Number 16 remembered the ledge, which protected him against direct German fire. "I landed on the eastern end of Omaha and was fortunate to be where the sandy dune line was replaced by a rock formation that gradually rose from a few inches to over a hundred feet high." Soon the position was protecting many soldiers and later in the day would become an aide station to treat the many wounded on Fox Red.

On the beach, another D-Day hero was playing an important role in the attack on WN 60. Lieutenant Jimmie W. Monteith was responsible for the sup-

porting fires of the impending attack, directing the 75mm guns of two medium tanks from the 741st Tank Battalion into the German defenders. In addition, machineguns were set up to cover the assault force's advance. At 0900, Company L had a strong force positioned to attack the Germans from the rear. Cutler called for the naval gunfire to be lifted as his men advanced, using Satchel charges to destroy the concrete positions and their rifles and grenades to eliminate the rest. Quickly Company L was able to overwhelm the German defenders, taking thirty-one prisoners and opening the F-1 Draw. This would be the first *Widerstandnester* declared destroyed, opening a route inland.

From the water's edge, a veteran reporter for *Collier's Weekly*, Ernest Hemingway, considered too valuable an asset to be risked on the beach, observed Company L advancing inland from an LCVP. "Slowly, laboriously, as though they were Atlas carrying the world on their shoulders, men were (climbing). They were not firing. They were just moving slowing…" This was perfectly understandable, as German snipers and machinegun nests behind the beach continued to take a toll on the advancing Americans.

Company L turned west toward their original objective, the E-3 Draw. After destroying WN 60, they were well positioned to support the attack of Captain Dawson and Company G, advancing south toward Colleville. Later they would be joined by a section of Company K and M and ordered to move to flank the town through the village of Cabourg, which was located further east. In this advance they were struck by a determined German counterattack, and brave Lieutenant Monteith would be killed.

His heroic efforts on June 6 would earn him the second Medal of Honor awarded for the action in Easy Red. His citation would read in part, "Completely exposed to the intense fire, 1st L. Monteith led the tanks on foot through a minefield and into firing positions. Under his direction several enemy positions were destroyed."

WN 60 provides an exceptional view of the entire stretch of Omaha Beach to the west. It can be reached by turning north from the coast road at the tiny cluster of homes known as Cabourg. When the road comes to a "T", turn right and follow the gravel road to its end at the wooden barricade. Follow the path past the barrier to the open field, which is WN 60. There are two easily identifiable Tobruk mortar positions facing west, a command bunker overlooking the Bay of the Seine, and an antiaircraft position in the middle of the field. Like the other German defensive positions, WN 60 was encircled with barbed wire barriers and mines.

Opposite: The cross of Lieutenant Monteith, stands out with the letters picked out in Gold at the cemetery.

Fox Red.

At Colleville-sur-Mer, below the hamlet of Cabourg and WN60, the 6th Naval Beach Battalion set up a first aid post sheltered by the chalk cliff and right below the German defended position, at circa 0720. The war correspondent Taylor took a set of exceptional shots which were most evocative of the horrors experienced on Omaha Beach. Printed here are some of the photos showing men of the 3rd. Battalion of the 16th RCT. (1st Inf. Div.).

1. Aid men installed themselves by the shingle bank in the middle of the debris : here they are giving a transfusion.

2. Further on a doctor captain and other medical orderlies are also giving a transfusion to a wounded man covered by a blanket. His head is resting on a life belt used as a pillow.

Above: an orderly giving first aid to a wounded man whose expression is still marked by the terrors he has seen.

Opposite: an orderly filling out the wound report card for a man with bandaged head.

(DAVA, ETO-HQ-44 series 4778. Coll. Heimdal)

Medics

Medic's helmet shell and liner.

Other wounded awaiting evacuation having received first aid. Three of them have suffered head wounds. Between 6 and 18 June, 11.25% of the wounds were to the head. (DAVA, ETO-HQ-44 series 4778. Coll. Heimdal)

1. Tourniquet

2. Medical officer's instrument case.

3. Case for medics or doctors containing instruments and first-aid dressings.

4. Booklet of labels for the evacuation and transfer of the wounded.

(Fonds Fantastic Attic/Bayeux.)

Summary

The assault on Omaha Beach on D-Day is the story of the heroism and determination of the individual soldiers and the military principle of "mass." Despite tremendous sacrifice, young men continued to pour onto the beach until the force ratio was overwhelmingly in favor of the Americans. Their losses, however, were staggering. The 1st Division suffered 1,346 casualties with 871 coming from the 16th RCT. The 29th Division would lose 1,272 members of its organization, 1007 in the 116th RCT, with 247 of these listed as killed in action, a staggering 107 from Company A, nineteen of which came from the town of Bedford, Virginia. Suffering the worst per capita loss; this small community has become the site of the National American D-Day memorial. Per unit losses were the worst in the SETF where 111 of the 272 who landed or almost 41% became casualties. V Corps reported the loss of sixty-nine tanks during the day. In all, the American losses on Omaha Beach on D-Day including the Navy and Air Corps, amounted to 4,720.

The evening of D-Day found the V Corps headquarters near the beach just east of the E-1 Draw. The 1st Division would set up their CP, Command Post, further south in E-1 near St. Laurent with the 741st Tank Battalion nearby. The 29th Division CP was located in a gravel quarry near the beach in E-1. The 743rd Tank Battalion set up a 360-degree perimeter in the draw and conducted resupply operations in preparation for D+1. Units from both V Corps' Divisions were positioned south of the coast road prepared for the impending German counterattack. Men and materials continued to be offloaded on the beach throughout the evening. Final numbers for the day show 34,200 men and 100 tons of supplies were placed onto Omaha Beach.

The German units defending the beach would suffer over 1,200 casualties, five hundred of which were listed as missing in action; many of these had become prisoners of war. The loss of equipment was equally devastating, and in the afternoon of D-Day their resupply capability was practically nonexistent. The German Navy, *Kriegsmarine*, had little impact on D-Day other than limited E-boat and U-boat attacks. The absence of the famed German *Luftwaffe* caused Chief of the American Air Corps, General Henry "Hap" Arnold to call them the "They Left Waffe." The 352nd Division fought desperately on D-Day and beyond awaiting the arrival of the heralded Panzer Corps promised, but American fighter attacks took a heavy toll on any counterattack efforts.

Arriving on Omaha Beach D+1, war columnist Ernie Pyle writing for "Stars & Stripes", described the scene. "Submerged tanks and overturned boats and burned trucks and shell-shattered jeeps and sad little personal belongings were strewn all over the sands. That plus the bodies of soldiers lying in rows covered with blankets, the toes of their shoes sticking up in a line as though on drill. And the other bodies, uncollected, still sprawling grotesquely in the sand or half hidden by the high grass beyond the beach."

Opposite: The American cemetery. (G. Bernage).

Until well into the afternoon the beach was still being fired on by the 105 and 150mm guns of the 352nd Artillery Regiment as is show in this photo taken by the Coast Guards.

Stores brought ashore, ammunition boxes and jerrycans in the foreground, mixed up with miscellaneous debris.

The tank "Ceaseless" of C Company of the 743rd Tank Battalion abandoned on Dog Red, photo taken on the evening of 6 June. (NA/Coll Heimdal).

"In this shoreline museum of carnage," Pyle went on, "there were abandoned rolls of barbed wire and smashed bulldozers and big stacks of thrown-away lifebelts and piles of shells still waiting to be moved."

After visiting the beach several days later, British General Bernard Law Montgomery would write of his shock at what he saw. "If you saw Omaha Beach, you would wonder how the Americans ever got ashore."

Ernie Pyle writing for « Stars and Stripes », described the scene of devastation on Omaha Beach.
Below: The National Guard Monument on WN72. (G.B.)

Captain Charles Cawthorn, Commanding Headquarters Company of the 2nd Battalion, 116th RCT on D-Day and a newspaperman after the war, wrote in his book *"Other Clay,"* the detailed preparations the 29th Division had made. In the end he wrote, "It all came down to this brief first day of battle on the coast of Normandy, and, for so many of them, it all ended. For the rest of us, what has been since has not been the same."

Captain Archibald A. Sproul, who commanded Headquarters Company of the 3rd Battalion on D-Day and would be the last commander of the 29th Infantry Division before its colors were rolled temporarily in 1965, would write, "No men in the history of our armed forces ever fought with more valor or determination against such overwhelming odds than these men."

During this longest day of 1944 in France, America's "Greatest Generation," created the opening which would restore peace and freedom throughout the world. Lieutenant General Omar Bradley possibly summed it up best: "Every man who set foot on Omaha Beach that day was a hero."

The words engraved in the memorial wall in the Lorraine American Cemetery in St. Avold are so applicable to what was accomplished on D-Day, on that stretch of sand, on the Norman coast of France, that will forever be known as "Omaha Beach."

"Here we and all who shall hereafter live in freedom will be reminded that to these men and their comrades we owe a debt to be paid with grateful remembrance of their sacrifices and with high resolve that the cause for which they died shall live."

Captain Charles Cawthorn, commanding Headquarters Company of the 2nd Battalion, 116th RCT on D-Day. (116th Foundation.)

Brig. General Cota, Assistant Commanding Officer, 29th Division (left), and Brig. General Charles D.W. Canham, Commanding Officer, 116th Infantry, get together somewhere in the European Theater, 1946.

Glossary

AK : *Armee-Korps*, German Corps

AR : *Artillerie-Regiment*, German Artillery Regiment

CP : Command Post

DD : Duplex-Drive, amphibious tank

DUKW : Amphibious truck

ID : Infantry Division

LCA : Landing Craft Assault

LCM : Landing Craft Mechanized

LCT : Landing Craft Tank

LCVP : Landing Craft Vehicle and Personal

LSD : Landing Ship Dock

LSI : Landing Ship Infantry

LST : Landing Ship Tank

MG : Machine Gun *(Maschinen-Gewehr* in German)

MP : Military Police

USCG : US Coast Guard

WN : *Widerstandnest*, German Strongpoint

Achevé d'imprimer sur les presses de l'imprimerie de Champagne à Langres (52) en mai 2014
Georges Bernage, éditeur